Religion vs Spirituality – One Psychic's Point of View

Shirley Scott

BALBOA.
PRESS
A DIVISION OF HAY HOUSE

ISBN: 978-1-4525-4618-6 (sc)
ISBN: 978-1-4525-4619-3 (e)
ISBN: 978-1-4525-4617-9 (hc)

Library of Congress Control Number: 2012901641

Balboa Press books may be ordered through booksellers or by contacting:

Balboa Press
A Division of Hay House
1663 Liberty Drive
Bloomington, IN 47403
www.balboapress.com
1-(877) 407-4847

Because of the dynamic nature of the Internet, any web addresses or links contained in this book may have changed since publication and may no longer be valid. The views expressed in this work are solely those of the author and do not necessarily reflect the views of the publisher, and the publisher hereby disclaims any responsibility for them.

The author of this book does not dispense medical advice or prescribe the use of any technique as a form of treatment for physical, emotional, or medical problems without the advice of a physician, either directly or indirectly. The intent of the author is only to offer information of a general nature to help you in your quest for emotional and spiritual well-being. In the event you use any of the information in this book for yourself, which is your constitutional right, the author and the publisher assume no responsibility for your actions.

Any people depicted in stock imagery provided by Thinkstock are models, and such images are being used for illustrative purposes only.
Certain stock imagery © Thinkstock.

Printed in the United States of America

Balboa Press rev. date:1/30/2012

Acknowledgements

I want to thank Skip who is always there when I need him and a friend I would never want to be without. He has helped guide me through this book and played devil's advocate to keep me from wandering too far from the subject. I owe him a lifetime of thanks and dinners.

I also want to thank Danielle who read and reread this book to help edit it and was very patient with my changes and changes and changes. She is a very dear person who I'm lucky to have in my life.

Liane is another person who has helped me in so many ways. She has a warm and loving heart for all animals and it has been a big help in supporting my rescue ranch. Thank you for reading the book and doing some of the editing and giving me your ideas too.

There are many others who inspired me to write this book. Many were teachers in my past and others were just people on the street that I watched and learned from. In many ways, the world was my teacher and the people were the actors that showed me life is but a play. I acknowledge all their parts in this book and thank them.

About the Author

In 2000 I had a near-death out-of-body experience and when I recovered, I realized I'd brought back the power of clairvoyance with me. This experience changed my life and was the most wonderful thing that could have happened to me.

Since that time, I've been doing readings on both animals and people. I connect with loved ones who have crossed and find this connection helps people who are grieving.

I help people to empower themselves and start living a happier, less stressful life by seeing the truth about who they are. I believe that Spirituality should be simple to understand and live.

I teach classes on animal communication, psychic abilities and the paranormal as well as being the dog trainer for the "Dogs in Prison" program at the Washington State Penitentiary.

I have written several articles for Animal Wellness Magazine and other publications and I've been interviewed by several TV stations, on several talk radio shows and I have just published my first book, How Old Are We.

I have a 501c3 animal rescue that helps feed and find homes for unwanted and abused animals. I do workshops and speaking engagements on animal communication, animal behavior issues, the paranormal and living a spiritual life. I work with groups or individuals to teach people how to become more in tune with their pets. Everyone has a natural ability to communicate telepathically with an animal or other humans; it's something that is built into each of us. Please visit my websites at www.animaltalkhealing.com or www.animalrescueranch.com to find out more.

My new CD, "Face your Fears, Change your Life" is now available on my website.

Blessings

Shirley Scott

Preface

As you read this book, remember the content is my opinion. It's not supposed to talk you into any belief system, but I hope it will make you look at what you've been told to believe and examine those beliefs to see if it's working for or against you.

My other intention in writing this book was to take some of the "woo-woo" out of both religion and spirituality. My prayer is that after you read it you can see how even a small change in your life can make a big difference.

None of us can change the world by ourselves, however, if we change our personal world, it can affect the whole world. If we can find happiness, joy, love and peace in our personal world, we can help make a world of difference.

Maybe one day we'll learn that judging someone for what they believe is a waste of our time and energy. Also trying to convert others into your beliefs is rude and invasive. I hope one day we can live side-by-side without hate, fear or judgment.

This was the intention of the book. I hope you enjoy it and when you're done you'll think about your life and make some positive changes.

Chapters

Life

Life is very simple. We're born, we live our life and we die. What could be simpler? Oh, of course – it's all that "stuff" between birth and death. All those emotions and belief systems we have to learn to do something with. It's all the hard times and the good times that help form our belief systems and fill us with emotions. It's all the work, the play, the joy and the sadness that makes us who we are.

Being human isn't easy and we never seem to get used to it no matter how many times we re-incarnate. I believe we never get used to it because every time we come back, we have a new body and a new brain. After all when we die, we leave these things here. The only thing we take with us is our souls, which really are energy bodies. So with each incarnation, we are in a different time and have to adapt to whatever is going on in that era.

Life is an ever changing event. Every second there's a change of some kind somewhere. Most of us only see or acknowledge changes in our world or life, but they are happening all over the world and out into the universe and solar system. However, many humans don't see beyond the end of their noses and that's okay, but they have a very limited concept of life.

Life is more than breathing and going to work everyday. Life is growing, changing. We do this every lifetime and every lifetime we bring some of our last lifetime with us into the present one. Some of our old beliefs and lessons will come forward too. They remind us we have already learned something or give us a remembrance of how to deal with a situation.

We bring this knowledge, which is locked in the memory of our soul, forward to help us live a better life. Little by little as we live, many of us remember things from the past. We remember a town, that in this lifetime we have never visited yet know all about it. We remember a person, but don't know how. This is our soul helping us in this life time.

Most humans have a drive that takes them through life but they never understand what that life is really all about. They don't understand it's supposed to be fun and a place to experience and learn. All kinds of belief systems and judgments get in our way before we are even out of diapers.

Humans are a strange species, they don't act or think like other species here on Earth. We are driven by a different DNA pattern. Humans question everything that happens to them and everything that doesn't happen to them. They question the whys, the what ifs, the what fors and the who done its.

We want to study and explore everything but ourselves. Most other animals on this planet could care less about what another species is doing and why they're doing it. They're too busy in their own world doing what they're supposed to be doing to worry about someone else. That doesn't sound like us humans at all.

We not only want to know what makes all the other species tick, we want to know what our neighbors are doing and why. Don't you think we'd be more productive about our own lives if we just focused on it? I don't mean to ignore everyone or everything that's going on around you, but observing it and getting involved are two completely different things.

When we observe what is happening in our life and who we are or who we're becoming, we really start to live our life. We start to look at who we are and where we're going. We also start to see what we like or don't like about ourselves. We see changes, we see obstacles and we see miracles.

However, very few of us ever question why the sun continues to come up every morning or set at night. We don't question why the moon is full sometimes and then it can't be seen by the naked eye in only a few days. We take these things for granted and because science has seemly said this the way it's supposed to be, we believe it. We don't question why a bridge doesn't fall when we're crossing it, but we do question if there's a greater power than us out in space somewhere.

Humans make life so complicated it's hard to see the real truth about it. Dogs don't ask why they're a dog. Cats are just cats and they know it. Ducks know they are supposed to like the water and quack. All animals and plants do what their DNA and cellular makeup tells them to do or be. Humans, on the other hand, want to know why they're human and what they should do about it.

The best thing we can do is to pay attention. By paying attention to what we're doing instead of what everyone else is doing will make a big difference in your life. I'm talking about looking at the choices you are making and what direction you want your life to go in. I like to call it "stepping off the stage".

Stepping off the stage is taking a step back from your busy life and looking at what is happening. It's like being the producer of a play. You are the actor most of the time but to really take control of your life, you have to become the producer, the writer, the editor and the actor. You need to make all these jobs come together in one organized and grounded way.

Stepping off the stage is looking at the choices you made throughout the day or even the week. Stepping off the stage can give you a better look at where your life is headed before you get there. It's looking at the choices you are making and where they are taking you. It also gives you an opportunity to change your life by making new choices.

Stepping off the stage and looking at your life needs to be done on a regular basis, not just once a year. You need to become conscious of your choices and how they are running or ruining your life.

I love the saying, "if it's not feeding you, it's eating you". So many of us live like this and wonder why we're unhappy. We can be our own best friend or our own worst enemy. We need to look at what we are doing to ourselves and change it. Many times we blame others but if we are in a situation where it's painful or sad or it makes us angry, we need to look at ourselves and find out why. Then we need to heal it, change it and move on with the lesson we are learning.

Too many of us get caught in drama and think we have to live there. Look at how many people just follow their dreams and walk through the fear of the unknown and have it work out fine. This is what life and living are all about. Nothing holds us back more than fear and blaming others for our situation; remember, you have nothing to fear but fear itself.

Sometimes following your dreams can mean jumping in something new with both feet. It also means looking at where you are jumping and making sure it's on solid ground. Doing research and looking into a situation is only common sense. It's gathering information so you can make a wise choice. However, some of us analyze things to death and miss opportunities.

For example, say we're in a job we hate and want to quit but are afraid of walking away because we need the money. Many people say, "But I need the job right now." Okay but are you looking for another one while you are suffering in the wrong job? Remember if it's not feeding you, it's eating you. Jobs are things we can manifest if we really want to. I have manifested several jobs in my lifetime and they all fed me until it was time to move on, then I got out of them and moved toward something better.

I'm not saying it's easy but we can't learn anything really important unless we experience it in some way. Getting out of something that's painful and into something comfortable can create fear but walking through this fear is worth it in the long run. It's empowering and confirms just how powerful we really are. When we walk through fear, we start looking at life in a different light.

All the fear we live in has been around for thousands of years. No one really knows when it all started but it lives through what we believe. If we are afraid of trying something new, we will never grow. Our parents put fear in us about sex, doing well in school, doing wrong and being punished for it and many tell us to even fear God. That's a lot of fear.

I had a dream many years back but I remember it like it was last night. I was sitting at a picnic table eating when I realized someone was sitting across from me. I looked up and there was death – a black robed, dark figure without a face. I wanted to run. I started to get up to make my exit when all of a sudden I had this over-whelming feeling of sadness. I realized how sad death was and no one loved him. I reached across the table to cradle his unseen head in my hands and said, "I love you." He disappeared and I woke up.

The message I received from this dream was that if you walk through fear with love, the fear will disappear. Many belief systems teach us this but then they tell us to fear our Creator. They tell us he will punish us if we aren't good. This is nuts!

If you have read my book, How Old are We, you would have read about my theory on the "master plan" of the universe. It's simple. We can't fail. We are made to succeed no matter what we do. If we do something and it turns out wrong, then we've just learned what not to do. If we do something and it turns out right, then we've learn what to do. It's as simple as that. We make life too complicated because we put fear into everything.

When we start stepping off the stage, we're making our life simpler. We're looking at everyday events and choices. We see where we're going or what our choices are or where these choices are taking us. We're focusing on us. This will help us recognize when we are giving someone else our power. It'll help us to see if we're living our life or if we're trying to live someone else's. It'll help us see where we need to make corrections and what we need to leave out of our lives. It's simplifying your life so you can enjoy it more.

When we do this we are taking control of our thoughts, words, and actions. It's empowering you to be your true self. Because it empowers you, you face your fears in a more positive way and see they shouldn't be feared but welcomed as a challenge and opportunity to learn something.

Life is supposed to be fun and magical. It supposed to be a learning adventure and, even though it's hard at times, it doesn't have to be a nightmare. Hundreds of thousands of years ago when we first came to Earth, we knew the way the Universe worked. We carried the secrets in our energy body and they really weren't secrets, they were just the rules of the energies that run this Universe. It was a way of life, it was natural, and it just was. We worked with the rules and the energies so we created many things.

Then we became human and everything changed. We started raping Mother Earth and her plants and animals. We over killed for greed and we thought everything would stay the same, but nothing stays the same, especially when we change the energy around something.

Greed and fear took over humans and here we are today still trying to get back to the times of balance and knowing. The good news is we'll get there; but the bad news is it's going to take many more generations and thousands of years because we have to "get over" ourselves first.

The first humans knew the gods and what they were capable of doing. These humans also knew they were part of these gods. However, the gods lived in a different dimension and had no human bodies. It was easy for the gods to create. The problem humans had was the human body was heavy. This heaviness meant it was harder to manifest physical objects.

This was the first fear. Not being able to manifest as quickly as we would like. This fear created the fear of low self esteem. The first humans didn't understand the time lapse on Earth between the dimensions of thinking something and manifesting it. When we are just energy bodies, we think it and it happens, not so when we are human. If we didn't have a time lapse, our thoughts would manifest in a second and we'd probably regret it. An example is thinking it would be nice to have a pony and have one instantly appear in your front room.

When we became human, we also seemed to forget most of the knowledge of the universe. I blame this on our brain because it is part of the human body and not part of our soul. Our soul holds the knowledge we have of the ages and the lives we have lived, not the human body. Our brain has a lot of room in it for storage and I view it as a computer. We can store a lot of files in a computer but most of the time we forget where we stored them or what we named them so we can't find them. This is what we do with our brain in many cases.

Our energy body or soul can download our knowledge to our brain but then we have to have an experience to open the file. It's like a certain experience is the title or name of the file. When that experience happens, the file opens and we start remembering things. We need to learn to access our storage files better and really believe they are what they are when we do access them. Most people think it's their imagination or they're crazy but many times they're remembering and bringing those memories forward. Before we were human, we had this knowledge and were very much in touch with the forces that rule this universe.

No one seems to know when the human ego took over but when it did, humans lost touch with the natural forces of the universe. Many think this happened eons before Atlantis. I know Atlantis hasn't been proven or found yet, but we are just beginning to explore the oceans and the all mysteries and secrets they hide. I believe everything will be discovered and uncovered when the time is right. Even though Atlantis maybe a myth or legend right now, there is always some truth in the myths and legends of the past.

Before I go into this next couple of paragraphs, I have to explain something. As my scientific friend says, "None of the stories about

Atlantis can be proven and they are just a part of Greek mythology." Okay, but many myths have some truth in them and are based on something other than thin air. Many stories in the Bible are now being questioned because there seems to be no scientific basis from them either; but we still believe them.

So please bear with me on the following and until Atlantians and Lemurians can be proven or disproven beyond any doubt, let's just let our imagination fly and have some fun with it. After all, when we all die and go home, we'll all learn the truth and have a good laugh no matter what the truth or myth might be. So here goes with some theories and/or myths or whatever you would like to call them.

It's thought by many that Atlantians started out with good intentions. They seemed to have a high intelligence and it's rumored they built a wonderful city. Many say they were a very advanced civilization and had flying machines and underwater ships. They were supposed to have been able to work with the unseen forces here on Earth to levitate, use telepathy as communication and other works we think are now impossible. This could have been possible if they were the descendants of some of the first energy shape shifters who came to Earth.

If they were descendants of the shape shifters, they would have been new at this Earth thing called gravity. They could still have had the knowledge to work with the natural forces on Earth and in the sky but might have forgotten them when they became human.

It's said the Atlantians powered their cities with crystals. Even today we use crystals in our radios and computers for good reasons. First, they don't expand much when heated. Second, they can change shape slightly when they are subjected to an electric field. This phenomenon is known as the piezoelectric effect. All crystals have their own natural vibration or pitch. If you hook an alternating circuit to a crystal and tune the circuit's frequency to the crystals' natural frequency they will both resonate. Each crystal's pitch or vibration is determined by its shape and size. The Atlantians seemed to know this and used it to their full advantage.

They had one main crystal that was supposed to be powerful enough to run energy through the city. This crystal was thought to be several thousand feet high and so big around you would need 100 people holding hands to encircle it. Up until recently, many people thought there were no crystals this big anywhere on Earth. However when the crystal caves in Mexico were discovered, it proved there are giant crystals and Atlantis could have had one as their power source.

The problem was the Atlantians wanted more control and power over Earth and the people who lived in the city. No one knows when this shift in thinking took hold but I'm sure it was because their humanness started getting the best of them. I think greed and fear are human conditions and we need to heal these conditions as much as we need to find a cure for cancer.

Anyway the Atlantians turned the pitch of the crystal up to get more power. No one is sure why or how much more power the Atlantians wanted, but they wanted it and that was all that mattered. Sounds a lot like today's society, doesn't it?

The first time they did this, they had earthquakes and part of their island fell into the sea. They should have learned something from this action, but then again, they were as human as you and me and sometimes it takes us awhile. So they turned it up again, thinking the part of the island that fell into the sea was just a weak link. The earthquakes started again only this time they didn't stop. They had started their own destruction.

It's rumored that many Atlantians escaped in flying machines and ships before the island was torn apart and the ocean gobbled it up. I wonder if some of these flying machines came to rest right in the middle of other civilizations that were also on Earth at that time. I wonder if this is where some of the pictures on rocks and in caves of gods falling from the sky in ships came from. There's more than one civilization that recorded these flying machines around the same time in history so there seems to be some kind of connection.

These stories of flying machines and gods were handed down from generation to generation. Some of the real facts have been lost throughout time and the story telling. However, it's just like the Bible and its' stories, not all of it is as true as we would like to think, as history is now beginning to prove.

I do think there were other humans on the Earth at this time. I believe that many of these souls had come to Earth in different human forms. Let me explain.

The form of humans back then and even today has to do a lot with where you live on Earth. Back then, if a soul lived in a cave, they looked different from the people who lived in cities like Atlantis. If a soul wanted to experience living the forest of South America, they needed to be different to survive in that habitat.

Each land had its own weather, landscape and other factors that would have to be faced by humans, so the bodies had to be different to. Some had to have more hair for warmth and some didn't. Some had to be taller and some shorter. Some didn't need to speak and others had too. All these factors needed to be manifested into the human body and then changed as it evolved.

As the Atlantians went out into the world, they took their knowledge with them. I believe this knowledge is how some of the pyramids were built. Many studies are starting to show that pyramids around the world were built about the same time or very close to the same time with the same basic knowledge.

There is, of course, no proof the Atlantians landed in these lands and gave the people the knowledge to build these wonders of the world, but it does make you think. However, if it was the Atlantians, they must have shared their knowledge of building and how the universe works.

These gods from the skies, whoever they were, seemed to have the knowledge of magic and even life and death. They probably shared many secrets of the Universe that the other people didn't know. I'm sure mistrust, greed and jealousy grew, after all they were human. They probably began to feel more powerful and they wanted to control other people and the Earth. This of course was the beginning of the end for them just like it had been for the Atlantians and every greedy civilization from that time to the present day.

Many leaders of the ancient tribes and civilizations probably decided that only they should know the magical ways and hid the knowledge of the universe from others. As these leaders began to die, much of the knowledge died with them. Many of the leaders today don't know these secrets and are ruling only with ego and greed.

Before we had leaders, souls just came and went as they pleased. No one hurt anyone else. There was no need for control because every soul was experiencing what they wanted with out harm to anyone or anything. The soul only knows love, so there was no imbalance or control.

Ego and greed have a major control over most humans and they use them in the wrong way. It's going to take awhile before we can overcome what has happened to the human race. Even though we are somewhat better now than we have been, we still aren't perfect.

Remember, we are a very young species here on Earth and we have millions of years left to evolve. Even though we don't throw people to the lions anymore because it's no longer politically correct, we still torture, kill, lie, steal and do other nasty deeds to each other. I find it amazing what we turn into when we decide to take up residence in a human body.

It reminds me of people who are on a vacation. Many people think they can do anything they want in a place they don't live in because they think no one will ever see them again. Just look at how some people act when they are away from home. They drink too much, they party too hard, they over do casual sex and they think they own the town because they're a tourist. Is this an outward metaphor for what we humans are doing here on Earth? Are we on vacation from the other side and think we can get out of control and not pay any fines? Do we think we can litter, destroy, rape and pillage each other and Mother Earth, only to return home with no penalty? Wow, doesn't that shed a different light on how we live and how we should live?

So let's look at life, in a general way, to see how we fit into what is happening here on Earth. Everyone or everything on this Earth, and even in the universe, has a birth, a life and a death. There is nothing that doesn't do this. Nothing in this Universe, or in outer space for that matter, lives forever. The only thing that is promised to live forever is our souls. Many of the old civilizations on Earth seemed to either know this or believe this. They all had some kind of ritual for life, death and the afterlife.

Life as we know it seems to have more questions than answers. We seem to struggle and fight our way through life. We never quite feel we are winning, or if we do win, we feel there is something else to do, something to go after, something to create or live or achieve. This is life. We do it every day, day in and day out. That's part of our creative DNA.

The creative DNA I'm talking about isn't really in the human body, but in our soul, the real life force of our body. Without a soul the human body would be just another empty shell. Humans in general aren't very creative or active. The body is heavy and cumbersome. Gravity, stress and a lot of other outside influences affect the body in many ways. That's why it's good we have a separate force running us.

When we listen to our inner voice, which in most cases is our soul, we live better lives. However, we need to be careful about the voice we are listening to. Our ego will tell us we are either better than everyone else or worse than everyone else. Your soul says you're okay being who you are and you don't have to be better or worse. So listen carefully because your soul will make it simple. It just wants you to be a person who is creating good things for yourself.

I feel there's a master plan for each universe. Ours is to experience, create, grow and take that knowledge back home when we die. We can't fail. Humans are programmed to succeed. We just don't recognize it. From a very young age we listen to other people, their beliefs and thoughts and we start believing in what they believe in instead of believing in what we feel is right. We are re-programmed from a very young age to "try and fit in".

Our parents might say we can't do something. We take this in, we think it means we aren't good enough. That's the ego talking. This kind of thinking and listening to the ego gets us into trouble from the start. If we're told too often by our parents or classmates we can't do something, then we think we can't. This starts complicating our lives almost before we're out of diapers.

We start questioning what we can and cannot do. We grow up feeling not good enough to get what we really want. We stop trying because we feel we can't succeed at anything anyway, so why try. Many of us settle for something that doesn't fulfill our lives or what we really don't want to do. By the time we're grown ups, we wonder why we're not happy or feel incomplete.

We are supposed to be like children every day. That doesn't mean not to take responsibility for our thoughts, words or actions. It means explore, learn and create adventure. Start watching a child and how they look at their world. Every day is a new adventure and there's something to learn and something to create. We should always get out of bed in the morning with the idea that this is the first day of the rest of my life and how can I make it the most wonderful day I've ever experienced.

Look at problems as opportunities to learn and grow. Walk through them with the wide-eyed wonder of a child learning something for the first time. When others give you a hard time about something, look at the fact they might be jealous of you or they might not feel good about themselves and it really has nothing to do with you.

Humans seem to turn lessons into a drama. If we realized we're just living a life on this planet and we're here to learn something, it's simple. We don't own anything here because we can't take it with us. We are only borrowing everything for a short period of time. We're here to experience, see and grow. Then we go home with a great experience to share with others. The saying "life is only what you make it" is very true. If you want to live in drama, you'll live in drama. If you don't, you'll make other choices and go in a different direction.

It's hard for humans to let go of an idea, person, place or thing and walk toward another goal or in another direction. Humans want to analyze everything to death before they do this. We want to make sense of all situations and everything that happens. I think that takes the magic and fun out of life many times. We really never have control over anything but our thoughts, words and actions. Let's stop all the analyzing and let life be life.

When someone gives you a gift from out of the blue, what's the first thing that crosses your mind? "I wonder what they want from me." Maybe you think there are strings attached. Yes, sometimes there are but you can cut those strings. If you know a person is giving you something just because they want something back from you, you have the choice to take the gift or refuse it. If you take it, it doesn't mean you have to give them anything back. And you certainly don't have to feel guilty about not giving them anything in return. It's just that simple. It's their problem, their expectation, and their intent was wrong from the start.

A big part of life is learning to experience emotions without letting them rule or ruin your life. Emotions are not who we are, they are energy and therefore inanimate objects. We are the ones that make them into "things" that rule our lives. We can make emotions simple or we can blow them out of proportion.

Let's look at a few examples.

I'm going to pick jealousy because this is a big emotion in this world. Jealousy is a very wasted emotion. Jealousy is the fear of not being good enough. You feel you aren't good enough to have someone love only you. You feel you aren't good enough to have the "stuff" other people have. You're afraid you aren't good enough to have as many friends as other people. You're afraid you aren't good enough to get a better paying job. You're afraid someone is smarter than you or knows more. The list can go on and on. This is all jealousy.

If you can look at yourself and say, "I'm good enough to get whatever I'm supposed to have in this life time," it takes the jealousy away. I heard a story once about the Dalai Lama and jealousy and I'd like to share it.

He was speaking in English to a group of people when he couldn't think of the right word to use. He sat and thought for a moment and then his interrupter leaned over and whispered in his ear. He sat quietly for a moment and then said, "Oh, I'm feeling jealousy because my interrupter knows more in English than I do." Then he let out a great laugh and continued, "That's his job and he's very good at it. It's not my job and, therefore, I let my jealousy go and I'm thankful for his path in life."

That's experiencing an emotion, looking at why you are experiencing it and letting it go – all in about 3 minutes. He did not become the emotion. He didn't let it rule or ruin his life. He saw what was happening and let it go.

I tell people if their partner really wants to cheat on them, there's nothing they can do about it. Somewhere, somehow, that person will find a way to do it no matter what, so why waste your life energy on worrying about it. If a partner is going to cheat on you, get rid of them and let them get on with their life and you get on with yours. Look at what you learned from them and use it from that point forward. Don't hang on to it by talking about it or expecting the next person in your life to do the same thing. Really, let it go.

Life can be that simple as long as we don't hang on to our emotions. Many people who get a divorce never forgive their partners for it. That's a waste of time and a waste of your life and usually the other partner is having a great time not giving the divorce a second thought. That's what probably makes us mad. They don't seem to care they hurt us and they have moved on with their lives.

If you find this situation in your life, look at the lesson here. If you just let go of the hate and ill emotions you have for them, you can go forward with a new look at life. You too can start enjoying life with others. Remember we are in this game of life together and we are only here a short time to experience, learn and then go home. If you get stuck in the emotion, you aren't living life to it's fullest.

Life is supposed to be as simple as child's play. Being we are a very young species here on Earth, we do have some advantages; we still have millions of years to perfect not only the human body, but the emotions that run the human race. It takes generations to change how the world views something. The masses of people have to believe in the same thing at the same time, which isn't easy for us to do.

Look how long it's taken us to look at government, religions and other organized beliefs and start questioning if they're really working in our best interest. We're just starting to come out of the closet, so to speak, on these subjects because they aren't making us happy anymore. It'll take more time to change these things, but the good news is we have time. We have all the time there is in "forever and ever".

We have already been around forever, just not in the human form. We can look at fossils and rocks and figure out how long ago some forms of life started. We're starting to question the "ape to caveman" theory as we uncover more. I'm not saying we haven't evolved, but I have my own theory about where humans came from and how we are forever changing and evolving.

My theory says we were energy beings in outer space just traveling around in another dimension, having a good time visiting other universes and solar systems. The creative force that made this Universe and millions of others probably made us about 900,000 trillion years ago. We might have just been specks of energy that needed light and energy to start forming into our own energy being; just like the way universes need light and energy to form solar systems and galaxies. Looking at the way universes are formed is exciting but could it be a metaphor for the way we were formed?

If our souls are energy and light, then we should be a part of the same energy and light that's creating more universes in outer space right now. Is this the work of a god or gods? Or is it just energy manifesting its self in different ways? And aren't we manifesting some of the same kind of energy here on Earth? Does that make us mini gods with the power to do more than we think? Are we so young we're just starting to "grow into" our humanness?

Why are there other universes being created if this universe is the beginning or ending of anything? Do you think these universes are planned? Do you think they are timed just right so when our sun burns out they'll be ready for us to move into? Are we from another solar system and this galaxy was ready for us when we were ready for it? If so, who planned it that way? Are we part of that massive energy force? If we are, we would be wise to remember we aren't really human. We are energy beings living in a human body and somehow we are still connected to this force.

I believe we all came from this source because we have the need to create on a continuous basis. We might have just made a left turn at a stop sign while this creative force went straight. Maybe our free will lets us come here to experience all of this. Maybe we needed something to do, more to create and we picked Earth to do it on. Maybe we needed to create and experience different things, like children at play. Some of us decided to go to other solar systems to learn things. Others decided to stay here. Some of us might have watched this galaxy form and the more we watched and helped with the creation, the more we thought it might be nice to experience life here.

Yes, I said we helped. In Genesis God said, "Let us make man in our image." So who was he talking to? I feel it was us – as in "energy beings". We were here helping, however, we found as the gravitational pull on Earth grew we couldn't stay on Earth in our energy bodies. After all, as energy beings we are in the fourth dimension. Fourth dimensional beings can't stay in a third dimensional world, just like third dimensional beings can't live in a fourth dimensional world. Each can visit, but because the vibrations of each dimension are different, they can't stay unless they match the vibration of that dimension.

The human body has some of the elements of Earth so the body can live on Earth. The elements of Earth that are in all plants, rock, animals and humans, keep our bodies connected to Earth through their vibration. If we were Martians, we would have to have some elements of Mars so the body would match the vibration of Mars and we would be comfortable there.

It would only make sense that our bodies have to be part of Earth to live here. So I believe we had a hand in making who we are. We, as energy beings, will live forever but because the human body is connected to this dimension, it has to die. We are not supposed to be on Earth forever. We are supposed to experience, learn, grow and then go back to the energy world and share our experiences. This is what life is all about.

If we look at everything in this universe, nothing lasts forever. The plants, the animals, the rocks, everything dies. There are things that are renewable like air and water but even they can have their limits. While we're here, we get to explore all these physical elements that we soon take for granted.

So how did we start out? I think we were what many people call Lemurians. They were energy bodies that could come to Earth and shape shift into anything they wanted. This was probably millions or even billions of years ago when the Earth was younger and the gravitational pull was less than it is now; but that still doesn't tell us where we came from or how long we have been here.

There are no fossil trails of man that show us how we came to be. We have many other fossils that show us the timeline of many plants and other animals and how they evolved but we haven't uncovered anything like that for humans. There are some fossils that suddenly appear and date back about 200,000 years ago and just recently a skull of a woman has been uncovered which could be as old as 4 million years. It will be interesting to see what stories that will bring up in the world of religion and evolution.

Now don't get me wrong, I'm not against or for religion. I think it has its place in the world just like any other belief or club you join. But just like any other organization, religions have too many rules, too much dogma and too much power goes to a very few select people instead of helping people empower themselves. This is not living; this is being told what to believe and what to do.

Time is always changing and so is our outlook on life. We are uncovering new evidence of who we are everyday. We need to live outside the boxes that many organized "clubs" want us to live in. We need to update and change with the times and what is happening here on Earth now, not what happened thousands of years ago.

Religion has its place and, in most cases, it gives us a starting place to start thinking about who we are. The problem is we start to believe in everything it tells us and then we get lost in dogma and man-made rules we should live by. I think there is a need to understand there is something more powerful at work here and in space. I think this power is greater than humans, but I think we're part of that power. I also think it doesn't matter what you call it – it's all the same powerful force.

The foundations of many religions give us a starting point to understand many events on Earth that we call the paranormal; which is normal in my world. They teach us about angels, saints, God/Goddess, demons, devils and spirits that are around us. However, most of their explanations about where we came from just don't make sense to me. We know Adam and Eve weren't the first humans on Earth, so why the story?

Maybe there were humans here before Adam and Eve but they weren't as highly developed as the "God made" couple. Maybe they were introduced to the world to interbreed with the humans that were already here to make a superior human. Maybe this was part of our evolution. Or maybe the people that were already here were as highly evolved as many discoveries are starting to prove, and the Adam and Eve story was just a story to give power to an already misunderstood god.

In many cases, it seems that humans just walked onto Earth from another dimension. Some say this even proves the Adam and Eve story in the Bible. If all of a sudden man was here, then God must have made them. There is one big flaw in this story. The time line doesn't fit. Adam and Eve are thought to have been "made" about 4 to 6 thousand years ago. Science is proving there were thousands and hundreds of thousands of humans already living in different places on Earth by that time.

Many scholars of the Bible are beginning to view these stories in a new light. Many seem more like fairy tales of the past than anything else. Many believe the story of Adam and Eve was just the beginning of a few people taking control of the many. They believe the whole Adam and Eve story is more likely a nursery rhyme with lessons than the actual truth. Even if they did exist, they were "made" at least 90,000 to 120,000 years after the first human fossils were made. This would make it impossible for them to be the first man and the first woman.

Could God have looked at the people who were already here and just wanted to make improvements? Isn't that what we are still doing today? Could He have been saying to us, "We didn't do our best the first time and now we have to make a new and improved Human?" And isn't that we are still doing today? We are trying to tap into the DNA of humans to end disease and birth defects. Hell, even Hitler wanted to create what he thought would be a prefect race.

So Adam and Eve were formed. Their blood was not mixed with the other humans already on Earth. This might mean they had more of the power of the Creator or energy source in them. They might have been more like gods than the other humans on Earth who had mixed their blood with other humans for generations.

Adam and Eve might have been put here to reintroduce more of the "god" power back into the humans that were already here. Maybe we were forgetting who we were and where we came from and we needed a purer blood line to get back some of our power. Who knows, but that might explain one other troubling part of this story; where did Cain find his wife?

If Adam and Eve were the only humans, and they gave birth only to Cain and Abel and Cain killed Abel, where did the female come in? I've always wondered about that.

Another theory of how the human body was formed is that enough particles of the right amino acids, proteins and other elements to form a body bumped into each other and starting forming life millions of years ago. However, scientists estimate the chance of this happening is so great that the number is a 4 followed by all the zeros you could put down on a piece of paper that would stretch the length of our galaxy or beyond. So that's maybe a farfetched theory.

There's another theory that we were "dropped off" here, so to speak, by aliens as an experiment. Some say we came from a dying planet in another galaxy and when we evolved into humans, we forgot where we came from. This might explain why we don't have any human fossils showing evolution from apes to what we are today. It might also explain why we are so fascinated with outer space. There is no hard evidence for or against this theory.

Some say it was God who designed the human form and then another intelligent life form came and manifested it into the physical world. In other words, they created humans through their thoughts, just like we create things now through our thoughts. This could have been the Lemurians. Because the Lemurians were energy beings, it might be possible they saw the energy around the idea of a human body and manifested it.

It would be like us drawing an idea on paper and then taking the steps to build it. They might have taken several different attempts at this and that's why we have different looking people all over the world. Maybe the Lemurians saw the life force particles of protein and amino acids coming together and they had the knowledge to help them form life. Or maybe they were just experimenting and that's why we aren't perfect. After all, the Lemurians lived in a different dimension so their prospective of life and a physical body could have been flawed too.

The mystical shamans in South America had a name for this dimension where souls lived; Aluna, which means Mirror World. They believed man walked through this dimension and onto Earth. However man was unable to cope with things in this dimension and laid down to rest. As he slept, another energy being who had become human, came and placed psilocybin mushrooms on him and around him. When he woke, he found them and ate them. The mushroom's affect took hold of him and his brain and he clicked into action. He rose and walked off to find others who had come through the same Aluna doorway.

Terrance McKenna, the author of Food of the Gods, wrote about the mushroom activation story of the human consciousness but never talked about the "walk-in" theory of the Lemurians or other beings. More and more stories of "walk-ins" are being reported today but because there is literally no trace when it happens; it can't be proven or disproven. However it makes more sense to me than the other stories. When we start to look at the timeline of Earth and what we know today about when the first humans started to show up, the timing would be about right. Also, more and more people are saying they are "walk-ins" from a different dimension.

Walk-ins today say they have traded places with another soul in the same body. They say they had a contract with a soul and, at a certain time, the original soul leaves their body and the new soul walks in and takes over. It's the same body; just a different soul.

A few years ago, I had a woman come for a reading who told me she was a walk in. Her husband said she had changed so much overnight that he didn't know her anymore and wanted a divorce. She wanted a divorce too. She told me she had come to finish some work and he was in her way. It was a strange story but she believed it with every cell in her body and who am I to be the one to judge it right or wrong.

Okay so if beings once walked into our dimension from Aluna, they would need a body so they could stay on Earth. That body would have to contain some of the same elements and vibration of the Earth so they could stay here. This is where the mushrooms come in.

Once they had ingested the mushrooms from Earth, there would be trace elements of Earth in them. This could have been any food found on Earth but mushrooms have a lot of "Earthy" stuff on them and they grow from the Earth. This food would have lowered their vibration so they could become more solid and stay here. This may seem farfetched but we should remember that nothing on Earth is solid. Everything is moving with atoms and molecules; everything is really just very slow moving energy. So if this is the case, we should be able to slow down or speed up the movement of these atoms and molecules to walk into other dimensions if we really want to and vice versa.

If you start looking at everything on Earth and even Earth itself, you'll see that nothing is solid. Everything has slow moving particles of matter that vibrate at different levels. This is what "forms" objects here on Earth. We can form anything we want if we really believe it and work at it. There are Buddhist monks who can form a white ash in the palm of their hand out of thin air. Ghost can materialize before us and they're in a different dimension. We see things in energy that are in other dimensions, so this different dimensional theory is not that far out.

After all, our own science is forming bodies in test tubes and we are cloning everything. What's to say the Lemurians didn't do the same thing? We might be taking what they did and trying to improve upon it as we naturally evolve into higher beings.

When the Lemurians "formed" themselves into humans, they had to be wild with excitement at what they were experiencing. The human body could do so many different things they couldn't experience in an energy body. It must have been like being at Disneyland. Just getting used to the heaviness of the human body, and the all the different emotions they started feeling, had to be a ride all by itself.

If this theory is true and we really are energy bodies with some kind of connection to a different dimension, then we should be able to visit that dimension anytime we want to. This would also explain why some of the dreams we have seem so real. We are going into a very real dimension with our energy bodies while our human body sleeps. This could also be where we go when we die. When the human body dies, we can't stay in this dimension without a physical form at least not for very long.

Throughout time we have evolved and adapted to the changes and climates on Earth. We're a very smart and evolving species, believe it or not. We have evolved from what we used to be into what we are now. If you look around the world, you'll see why people who live in different climates and conditions look the way they do. You'll start to see why people are shorter in one geographical area than another; or why some people are heavier and some are thinner. It all makes sense once we step back from the screen and look at the whole picture.

One thing we know and understand for sure is that humans are a complex and underdeveloped species. We have a bigger brain than we seem to use – although I have some ideas as to why this is. I think much of our brain is used for storage of past lives.

The human body can have parts removed and live without them. We can replace parts and rebuild some; yet there are parts we can't live without or even regenerate. So the body isn't perfect and we still have things to work on. But we have time, and like I've said before, the human body isn't meant to live forever anyway.

We should enjoy life on Earth because this dimension is a wonderful thing. We have new and different experiences every day. We need to enjoy them more and see the wonder and change in them. We need to appreciate them. We take too much for granted. We don't enjoy the simple things enough. We think we always have to be busy but sometimes it's just nice to stop and really see what is happening around us.

Life is supposed to be a great opportunity to explore another dimension. We are always so intent on looking into the paranormal and other dimension - that's fine but remember to look at the dimension in which you are living. You'll be back in the other dimension you came from soon enough.

I believe the dimension we call the paranormal is where we came from and that's another reason we are so obsessed with it. The word "para" means beside or to one side. So the paranormal is a normal world beside us. It's another dimension where we can do different things than we can do in this dimension. It's not that strange in my thinking, just different. It means there is a parallel world which is beside you all the time. It never leaves us because we are part of it. Our soul or energy body is from that dimension. We are still connected to it, so it has to be with us. In my world, the paranormal is as normal as breathing in this dimension.

So where did we come from? Does it matter? What matters is we're here and we are supposed to be living life and enjoying it. Our ancestors meant for this experience to be simple. We come here, experience everything we can, and go home. There's no right or wrong about it. There were few rules in the beginning because we didn't need rules, but the human brain has evolved and so has the human condition we call an ego.

We now have the brain, the sub-conscious and the ego who all try to run or ruin our lives. We need to get back to "the simple" life. That doesn't mean to give up everything and go live in the woods. It means start simplifying your life by seeing that the stress isn't necessary. All the drama can go away. All the worry can be stopped if we really want to stop it.

There's a saying, "We are what we eat." Well, we are also what we think and what we do. All you need to do is change your thoughts and actions and see where it goes.

I had a client recently that wasn't happy with her life. She wanted to work with animals but she didn't know how to get started. She had an office job that was "eating her, not feeding her" and she wanted to do something else. I encouraged her to take the first step in living a happier life. That was to put ads in the paper that she was a dog sitter and dog walker. Her phone began to ring off the hook. She quit her other job and is now her own boss and very busy. She is happy and living the life she wanted to live. This is what life's all about.

If you aren't happy in your life, you aren't really living, you're surviving. The master plan of the Universe is a simple one - "You can't fail no matter how hard you try". We are set up for success; we just have to believe it. We have to walk it, talk it and do it. Nothing could be easier. Put the plan down on paper and start walking into your life just like the Lemurians might have walked into this dimension. Anything and everything is possible if you believe in it enough.

Why not go forward, from this day on, with the thoughts of a child discovering a new day. What can it hurt? Be surprised the sun came up. Be alert to the winds and how they change throughout the day. Study others and see how they act and handle their lives. Appreciate all the colors, smells, sounds and feelings. Let each one be new or a remembrance of a wonderful past event. Look at yourself in the mirror everyday and send love and grace to yourself.

There are other dimensions and things to explore, but remember where you are living now and enjoy all that is here around you in the present moment. We'll get the opportunity to explore other dimensions when we leave this one, so hold this very short time here close to your heart. Live in wonder and watch things unfold before you. Even our hard lessons will be easier through the eyes of joy. The children of the world prove this every day.

Life is only what you make it. Make it special. Make it magical. Make it whatever you want but do it in a positive way. Life is yours for the taking and living. The master plan is simple. Don't complicate it with becoming your emotions; feel them and then release them. Don't complicate it with fear and hate; live life with wonder and knowing. Let today be the day you let go of the things that are "eating" you and start to embrace the things that will "feed" you. And that means friends and family too.

Many people say, "Well if I know I'm going to come back, why do I have to be good? I'll just come back and live again and again." That's a good point but there are rules in this universe and one of them says what you put out you get back. So even if your karma doesn't get you this lifetime, it might in the next lifetime. Each lifetime should be better than the one before it. This is evolution of our souls.

Life is the evolution of our souls just like we are evolving to a better body, a better civilization, a better world culture. And just like it takes hundreds and maybe thousands of lifetimes to prefect our souls, it will take that long to evolve into humans who can embrace life and each other without fear, jealousy, hate, or greed.

Life is so simple and many of the great spiritual teachers repeated it over and over again. They all knew there were rules of the universe they had to follow as spiritual beings. They also knew there were laws of the physical world they had to follow because they were in the human body. They didn't always like either of these facts, but they found if they followed them, things seemed to just fall into place.

So stop putting out energy to complain about the physical laws and do something to change them. The laws can always be changed but rules of the universe are set in place to help us. If we work with these rules, we will find a happier life. Laws can make us unhappy but the rules of the universe are put in place to support us. If we're on the wrong path, things will appear difficult. We bitch and complain, but if we would get out of these unhappy emotions, we would see the universe is only trying to steer us in the right direction.

Don't let emotions get in your way. When something isn't going well, step off the stage and look at what you are trying to do. It might not be the right time or the right way, or maybe you really aren't supposed to do it. Don't judge it, let it go and do something else. Remember disappointment is an emotion. Don't be disappointed because the Universe is usually setting you up for something greater than you expected.

There are many souls on this Earth that are physically or mentally disabled and if you watch them, you will start to understand the true meaning of life. They are walking through their emotions every day. Most of them are examples to us of enjoying life to the fullest no matter what you are going through. They are some of the strongest souls we have here on Earth. I thank them everyday for showing me how strong a soul can be and how even the littlest things in life are supposed to be enjoyed. They are my heroes for sure.

So where did we come from and what is life all about? Does it really matter? We are here now and we'll be somewhere else later. That's life!

It's simple. Make it simple. Live simply, love simply, and don't get caught in the emotions. Step off the stage at least once a week to see what is really happening in your life. You are the only one that can make your life what you want it to be. You are the only one that puts yourself in situations that affect your life. You are the only one that can get out of the situations you put yourself in. You are the only one that really has control over your life. Don't give this power away to anyone or anything.

When you come to believe this with all your body, mind and soul, you will create miracles every moment of your day. Life is supposed to be a wonderful dreamland of adventure and creativity, not a nightmare. Wake up from your slumber and eat of the fruits of life. Walk away from the lies that say you aren't good enough to create a new life. Use the power plant you hold in your skull that we call a brain. Use the energy you hold in your heart we call love. Manifest your greatness without ego. Live your life as if each moment was your last and embrace the wonder of each minute.

This is life. Don't worry about the future because all you have is the present. If you make wise choices in the present moment, you have placed yourself right on the path for a wise future. Don't let life run you. Make choices with your free will and run your own life. Remember what you put out you get back. This is one of the unchangeable rules of the Universe. Learn to use it wisely.

Where's My Path- who am I?

Your path is a combination of your thoughts, beliefs, emotions and actions. It's as simple as that.

Many of my clients want to know what their path in life is. They feel they need to be doing something more or something different. Well, I tell them to look down at their feet and that's where they'll find their path. Your path is where you are. It could be an easy path or it could be a more difficult one; it depends on where you've placed yourself by the choices you have already made.

Choices are what make up your life and the path you're walking. There's really no wrong path but there are things you should try to avoid to help you stay on a happier, more productive path. Productivity is different in everyone's eyes but it should be something that helps you grow as a person. You should feel like you are accomplishing something. Please make sure it's positive productivity. You don't want to feel like you have gotten back at someone for doing something to you. That's called revenge and it will only get you bad karma.

Choices are how we create and walk our path. We create new things every day with our thoughts and actions. We can walk a different path everyday if we want to. We can change our thoughts and actions and that takes us onto a different path. If you think you're on the wrong path, than you need to change something in your life. Whether that change is your thoughts or actions isn't important, it's the change that's important.

Staying on your path is not walking the straight and narrow in fear of some kind of retaliation from an angry god. It's having fun. It should be a life of experiencing things. It's being conscious of who you are, of the sun in the sky, the moon at night and all the thoughts that go through your head all day long. It's being aware that positive thinking will bring you positive results and negative thinking will bring you negative results. It is being aware that life has much more to offer than you can even imagine.

We walk our path everyday no matter what we're doing. If we're on the wrong path, so to speak, we feel uncomfortable and things don't seem to go as we would like them to go. It's hard every day to see what we're supposed to be doing with our lives. If we're on the right path, life is easier and we seem fulfilled and happy; everything just seems to fall into place. We're surprised our life is going that well.

In my belief system, we all have to walk off our path at times to learn a lesson. We don't have to stay off the path but it can teache us a couple of things. First it teaches us we were on the right path to begin with and we should get back on it. Second, enjoy the right path when we're on it. Walking our path means always growing and learning. We don't have to save the world; we just need to make our world the best world we can. If we each did this, the whole world would be saved. We need to always start with ourselves before we go marching out to save anyone else.

Humans have the great gift of hanging on to the past and carrying around tons of baggage that doesn't serve us anymore. That just complicates our lives and really puts rocks and boulders in our path. The baggage we hang on too can ruin our lives. I've been through a lot in my life and if I would have hung on to even half of it, I wouldn't be who I am today. We're the ones that make the choices that complicate our lives and many times we block our own paths.

I don't believe God has anything to do with a lot of "stuff" in our lives. He gave us free will and let me tell you what I think that means. Free will is the biggest part of the miracle and/or mystery we create in our lives. Free will gives us the right to do what we want to do, when we want to do it. Free will is the only thing that will never be taken away from you. Even if someone is making the choices for you, you have the free will to go along or not go along with them.

Free will means I can come to Earth whenever I want and I can leave whenever I want. I can manifest jobs, kids, money, thoughts, actions and anything else I want too. I can do anything with my life because I have free will. God doesn't tell me when or what I should do because he knows something we should all know; our free will can make our lives wonderful or miserable and the choice is ours. Our free will is a precious gift and we should guard it as such.

Free will is something the ego loves to get control over. The ego will tell you that you can hurt someone with your free will. It tells you to run over people, think they aren't worthy of you and other egotistical things. Or maybe the ego will tell you your ideas and thoughts aren't worth anything and you need someone else to tell you what to do. This is giving your free will to others and letting them tell you what path to walk. It will never work for you.

Being a psychic, I can suggest a different path or way of doing something to my clients but it's always up to them whether they do it or not. I just know when they do, 98% of the time it works better for them. Remember even if I suggest something and they do it and don't like the outcome, the Universe had a reason or lesson for them to do it. Nothing is ever for nothing in this life. There's a reason for everything.

Free will means no one can step in and stop you if you really want to do something. Your spirit guides, your angels and everyone on the other side might be shaking their heads but you have the right to do it. Free will is something the human brain can't seem to wrap its self around and understand. It allows us to do anything we want whether it's good, bad, right, wrong, harmful or helpful. However, we should try to remember the one main rule of the Universe; what you put out, you get back. So we should use our free will wisely.

Let's look at a couple of examples to help you understand this rule and why it's so important. Let's say you use your free will to gossip about someone you really don't care for. You talk about them behind their backs to other people. Then in a few days you learn someone is gossiping about you and you wonder why. Well, here's the why – the Universe wants you to feel the same way this person feels when you gossip about them. Even if they don't know you said something about them, the energy behind your comments might have hurt them energetically.

People who judge people will be judged, because that's what they're putting out. People who hurt people on purpose will be hurt on purpose because that's how they've used their free will. People who bless others quietly and walk away will be quietly blessed and have miracles happen to them. People who help people will get help. People who control others will somehow be controlled by situations in their lives.

I think you get the idea of how free will works with the rules of the Universe. This rule is probably the most important rule to remember. This seems like a harsh law of the Universe but it can be used to help you find your path. If you follow what you want to do in life, work hard at manifesting it and do it so it doesn't hurt others, you will have it. It's that simple. We make it hard by putting all the "but what if's" into the mix.

We start doubting ourselves because, maybe up to this point, nothing has seemed to go right in our lives. Maybe nothing has gone right because we haven't been playing by the rules. Many people don't want to play by the rules and that's okay but it really doesn't get you anywhere. If you play by the rules, you can make the rules work for you. I'm not talking about man-made laws right now; I'm talking about the Universe and the rules that run it.

The rules of this Universe keep the sun rising and setting. They keep the planets in place and keep our Earth turning. They keep things running in a very organized way. Without the rules of gravity, rotation and a lot of other rules, we wouldn't be here. Everything has an order and law to it. If you start to understand this, you can make it work for you or against you. This is using your free will to help yourself and see what you want to do in life.

We all have something we came here to learn in this lifetime but how we learn, or even if we do learn anything, is up to us. God isn't going to step in and change it for us. We can ask for grace from the Universe and get it but that's another law. Ask and you will receive, just be careful what you ask for. Asking for something is governed by the same rule as "what you put out you get back".

Let's say you ask for a partner who will be rich and support you the rest of your life. Along comes this rich person and you get married because all you can see is the dollar signs. Once you're married, you find that person is very tight with their money and you're put on an allowance. Or maybe you find they're controlling about how the money is spent and what you can do with it. This is their free will and after all, it is their money.

You have just put yourself in a situation where you gave your free will away because of money. Remember money can make your life easier or it can make your life harder. Money is only as important as the energy we put into it. I know right now we're putting a lot of energy into it and we think without money we can't be happy but that's not true. Happiness is a thought form that money can't touch. I think you'll find if you stop worrying about money so much, it will flow better into your life.

I know when I get a bill for something; I just ask that the money be there to pay it. I don't worry about it, I just let it be. I used to be a worrier and my friends will tell you it took me a long time to see this and to overcome this fear. Then one day I stepped off the stage and looked at how my life had been going for the last ten years.

I saw that whether I had a job or not, I was always working at something to make ends meet and the Universe made sure ends were met. I never expected someone else to support me. I worked when I could at anything that was available. I was putting out the energy and effort and was being paid back by the universal rule of "what you put out, you get back." Money is just the end result of the energy you are putting out. It could be apples or oranges so just put the energy out there and see what happens.

When you really have the concept of free will in your back pocket, you can create any type of life you want to create. There is no stopping you no matter what obstacles seem to get in your way. You learn that these "obstacles" are really put there to make you think about what you are learning or what you're going to do next. Obstacles should be a welcomed opportunity to check in with yourself about what you are doing. Too many obstacles means stop and see what is happening and if you are doing the right thing. A few obstacles that seem to be easily worked out means you are learning a better way of doing it.

As humans we think if something isn't going well, it's not supposed to happen. That's not always the truth. Sometimes it's not the right time. Sometimes someone else has already done it and we are supposed to do it differently. Sometimes we aren't supposed to do it but we have to look at all the options. Step off the stage and look at what is happening.

Finding out our true path is hard because it can change with different stages of our lives. We start out as children and have different ideas as to what we want to be when we grow up. Some of us really work for that one job or thing we have wanted all our lives and some of us change our minds a hundred times. As we grow and learn things, our ideas change, our understanding of life changes and this is a good thing. I never thought in a million years I'd be a clairvoyant but the universe helped me to get on that path.

Let me tell you about my path in life so you can see how finding your true path can take many twists and turns.

When I was little I loved animals and loved to think there were fairies in my backyard, which I now know is true. I would bring all kinds of animals and insects home and my poor mother was always wondering what would come through the door with me. I wanted to be a zoo keeper and then a veterinarian until I realized I had to operate on animals and knew I couldn't do that. Then I wanted to be a model, which I did for awhile and found it was not for me.

When I was 18, I got married and thought about being a wife and mother and how wonderful it would be. My ex-husband had a two year old that we started to raise and then three years later, we had our son. I thought I knew what marriage would be like because I had a great example from my parents. I thought it would be blissful and wonderful and joyful.

It was long, painful and awful. My ex seemed to love his alcohol more than he loved me. He wasn't a very nice man when he was drunk. I stayed with him until my son was old enough to leave home and start his own life. I'll never forget what my son said to me as he walked out the door. "Mom, get out before dad kills you. I'm going to be fine. I want you to be fine too." I almost fell over.

After a few months, I kicked my ex out and I've never looked back. I was single at 46 and didn't have a clue what I was doing with my life. I had a good job and I put all my time and energy into it but I never felt like I fit in with the people I had to work with. There was something inside of me telling me there was something else for me to do. I didn't have a clue what it was and I wasn't on a spiritual path of any kind at that time.

It wasn't until the year 1999 that I started the path I'm on now. When I made the conscious decision to find my true self and what I was supposed to do in life, everything changed very quickly for me. I had a psychic reading, went on a spiritual retreat and then in 2000 had a near death out of body experience. It was like the Universe was picking me up and putting me in a new world. It was scary but I trusted my gut and followed the road signs I was seeing from the Universe.

I realized I was being lead to something else even if I didn't know what it was. Sometimes we just have to have faith that our choices are going to be the best for us no matter what. It's like driving in the snow or on ice at times. We need to know when it's safe to do it and when it's not safe. That's listening to our inner feeling and guidance or gut feeling or whatever you want to call it, but listening works.

After my near death experience, which brought me the gift of clairvoyance, I started dating a man who I really didn't like. I wondered why I kept dating him. I now look back at that time in my life and I can see what he did for me. He made me stronger in myself because he was somewhat of a control freak and stalker and I had to get strong to get rid of him. But the most important thing he did for me was to give me the chance to do readings on people when I was a beginning psychic.

Everywhere we went he introduced me as "his psychic girlfriend" and would ask if anyone wanted a reading. I was horrified! This is not what I had planned on doing the rest of my life. I didn't know what I was going to do because I had just lost my "good" job but being a psychic wasn't in the plans. I did give people readings if they wanted them and I was surprised at how good I was. It gave me enough confidence to go out into the world and start my own psychic business.

So you see, we really never know what is going to come our way. It's how we take what comes our way and use it to help ourselves that counts. That choice is part of our own free will. My belief system says there is no one looking over us telling us there is a path we must follow. We made up a plan before we came here and we try to follow it but birth is a trauma and it can make us forget our Earthly contract.

Sometimes we get side-tracked or "life gets in the way". However, no matter what life bring us, it's up to us to get back on a positive path so we can learn our lessons in a good way. We have angels and even other people who will try to help us but in the long run, it's always our free will and choices that create our reality and path.

I believe that God is way too busy to worry about what we're doing every minute of every day. That's why we have angels and spirit guides and a thing called our inner voice or higher self to help us look at what we are doing. Remember, these angels and helpers can be regular people or spirits that the Universe is sending us to give us a helping hand so we can't fail.

There's a universal rule that says you can't fail because this is a positive charged universe. Yes, I know it doesn't seem like it but it is. We're the ones that create the negativity. We're the co-creators of the universe and what goes on here. We are mini-gods unto our own selves.

Now I'm going to get a lot of flack on that one but really think about it for a minute or two. If we are spiritual beings that are pure energy when we aren't in the human body or any body for that matter, aren't we part of the same energy that is out there still creating more universes? And if we're part of that same energy on some level, shouldn't we be able to create many of the same things? It might be on a smaller scale because we have to deal with gravity and the human body, but we should be able to walk on water if we really wanted too. However walking on water is not high on my priority list. I'd much rather create a good comfortable life and help others empower themselves to do the same thing. That's what I'm creating by writing this book.

It has nothing to do with religion or believing or not believing in a god or angels or anything else. When you get right down to the brass tacks, it has to do with believing in yourself. That's what life is all about. Do you believe you can do anything you want to? Do you believe in your own power? Do you believe you can walk through this life alone, on your own with no help from anyone else and still be happy and create a good life? If you believe that, you have it. You have the true meaning of life and you will be walking your true path.

When we incarnate into the human body, we forget who we are and what we are doing here. It has to do with the human brain. When we're in spirit we don't have a human brain. The brain we have today wasn't with us in the last lifetime so it can't recall events of the past all by itself. That's why we have souls – to remember things from the very beginning.

I believe our soul is like a storage unit and everything is stored there. All our memories from past lives and what is happening today are stored for us to use later. Our brain stores everything from this lifetime but it can't store events from a past life because it never experienced them. It's our soul or energy body that stores everything then feeds it to our brain when we need the information.

When I started my path as a clairvoyant, I can remember saying, "I don't know any of this stuff. I'm so new at it."

One of my teachers turned to me and said, "No you're not. Just bring the knowledge of your soul forward. Remember who you are and walk the path you came here to walk." That really hit home.

I started changing the way I spoke to not only other people but to myself. I started saying, "I know this. I just have to remember." I started doing that every day with everything and my path began to become clearer. When I didn't think I knew something, I called on my inner voice and guidance as well as my spirit guides to assist me. The answers came and they helped guide me and they still do. After all, no one wants to go to a psychic that says "I'm new at this and I'm not sure about it."

An important thing we should try and remember about walking our path is to be who we are and live our truth. It's all about walking your truth, not just talking it. I can remember when I was first starting my spiritual path and was reading everything I could get my hands on about different spiritual ideas and methods. I read and read and soon everything was sounding the same and I found I was losing interest.

Before I went to bed one night, I looked up and said, "Now what? I've read and read and studied and listened but I don't feel I'm doing what I need to be doing."

It's funny how the Universe works. I laid down in my bed and just before I dozed off for the night I heard, "Live it."

I sat straight up and looked around the room. I started thinking and realized I wasn't living my path. I was reading about other people's paths. I was looking all over for the something I needed but I was looking on the outside and not the inside. I realized during the day when I was at work, I was a different person from the one that was living in my house by night and on weekends. I realized my job was not what I wanted to do and it was no longer fulfilling. I realized I was talking about spiritual things but I wasn't living them.

This was the start of becoming more conscious about what I was saying, doing and thinking. Once I started living my life consciously and taking responsibility for what I was doing, my life started changing. I started talking to my angels and spirit guides – even though at that time I had no idea who they were – and stopped reading so many books about what other people were doing. I started looking at what I wanted to do to make myself happy.

I went on a spiritual retreat and had so many miracles happen I thought I had died and went to a magical land. I still find it exciting when I remember all of it. It really helps to keep me on my path and in my belief system. I learned so much about myself, it was almost scary but yet wonderful. I had a near death out-of-body experience that brought me the gift of clairvoyance. I was guided to other psychics, visionaries and so many other spiritual people I was amazed. They just seemed to show up when I needed them. I lost the job I was beginning to hate and I moved to a small town to find out more about me. It's amazing what a small town can teach you. You either find yourself or you lose yourself. It was a great experience.

I feel I was guided and luck had nothing to do with what I'm doing today. I was given a gift and I continue to use it on my path every day. I'm not just living it anymore, it's who I am. I'm not perfect - no person or psychic is. We are all here to learn and do the best we can. That's the real life.

The fact still remains many people don't know what path they are supposed to walk. There are a couple of ways to find where you're supposed to be. One is to not only ask for guidance but to follow it when it comes. I have several clients that didn't follow what they wanted to do because of fear. They were afraid to quit their jobs and pursue what they really wanted to do. Now I'm not saying quit your job without researching and getting all the information about what you want to do first. We have to make informed choices, but fear shouldn't stand in our way.

Informed choices are wise choices. They show us what we can do and bring us the resources to do it. You may have a plan about what you want to do but your path might be bigger or better than you can imagine and the universe will guide you in a different direction. I wanted to be a writer for a long time. I wrote short stories and they were usually murder mysteries or some other grizzly story. None of them got published. I look back now and thank my guides for not letting them get published. That isn't who I am today. It took me years to get my first book published and I feel great about it.

Remember, life changes and we have to make changes to keep up with it. There are very few people any more that have the same job for 30 years like my father did. The times are faster now and people who don't change and grow will be put on a shelf – so to speak. The Universe and its' forces will force us to look at ourselves. That's what we are here for. To look, examine, and see what we want to learn. Our path is that of learning.

I see many people who were addicted to drugs or alcohol and now are on a totally different path. Many of these people are now helping others to get off this path of abuse. The now sober people couldn't really help others unless they have experienced it themselves. We can't even begin to feel what someone else feels about a situation unless we have gone through something similar. It's just not possible.

I have gone through sexual child abuse, cancer, a nightmare of a marriage, drug and alcohol education with my ex-husband and step-daughter, a divorce, a near death experience, had children and many other things that I can help others with. I've had a great life and since I've starting living my path, things just get better and better.

That doesn't mean I don't have my bad days or my down moods - I'm just as human as you are, but I get out of mine very quickly and look at it in detail. I look at what pushed my buttons and why; then I remove the buttons and move on. I don't just talk about what I do for a living, I'm that person and I do it. It took me several years to get here, but I never lost sight of what I wanted. The vision has changed a hundred times but the outcome is always the same. That's an important part of walking your path.

We walk our path to get to an end but when we get to the end, we start another path. I wanted to teach workshops on animal communication and paranormal events and it took about nine years but I'm doing it now. Those years brought me experience and more information than I thought my brain could handle. The information changed as the technology advanced and we found out more about the fourth and fifth dimensions and other "paranormal" happenings. So it was a blessing it took so long for me to become a teacher. It also gave me time to practice speaking in front of groups of people and to really become and believe in myself.

The way to start to see your path is to ask yourself what you really want to be doing. Remember the rules of the Universe say, what you put out, you get back. Start acting like the thing you want. Show the powers and forces of energy that we work with everyday what you want. Understand you are an energy force living in a human body but you can still make your life what you want it to be. No one can really stand in your way unless you let them. It's usually our own self that stands in our way. Sometimes we just need to step aside and let things happen.

I tell people to ask themselves, "What would I do if money and time were not important?"

If you say you would lay on the couch and watch TV for the rest of your life, you better think again. You could do that for awhile and then because you wouldn't be putting out productive energy, you wouldn't get productive energy back. You might even get negative energy back, like the TV going out and you not having the money to replace it because you haven't been doing anything. It could be a blessing in disguise because it just might get you off the couch and get you in touch with life and what you're really supposed to be doing. The Universe works in mysterious ways.

Really think about what you like to do, maybe you are doing it as a hobby now. Think about turning it into a job or something to make extra money. Many people don't want to turn their hobbies into jobs because then they think they won't enjoy them, and that might be true. So think about what brings you pleasure and how you want to make it work in your life. Don't be scared to ask or do something different because you can always change it later.

There's one thing I know, we're all teachers and we're all students. This is what we are here for. This is what we do on the other side when we die and bring our experiences to others. So why not look to teach someone something? Or look at something you have always wanted to learn and sign up for classes? Volunteer at something you love and see if it turns into something you can do for a living or see how it grows for you.

We all have gifts. Some of us just hide them very deeply because we are afraid someone might laugh at us or we won't succeed at it. You might be an artist or a pottery maker in your spare time. You might like to fly a kite and you're the best kite flyer around. Teach others how to do it and show them why you're so good at it.

You could be a guide in the wilderness, a swim instructor, a tutor, a music teacher, healer, a writer, a speaker and the list goes on and on. The list is as long as what you think. Pick one and take the step toward. This way the Universe will know what you want and will let you know if it's right for you. You'll know very soon which way you're supposed to go by how events in your life are going. We all need a creative outlet because we have DNA that screams at us to create.

Creating is how we learn, how we grow, and how we find out who we are. No matter what we are doing or creating, we are experiencing something and growing in some way. The growth can be positive or negative; the choice is up to us, just remember that your choices can affect others. We are all connected in some way. Even if you don't believe we came from the same energy source a trillion years ago, we are all on this Earth now and so that makes us Earthlings and connected to what happens here. So creating in a positive way only adds to the positive energy as a whole.

Humans have seen their possessions come and go and we still haven't learned they aren't ours to keep. It's not about the biggest house or how many cars or toys you have; it's about living your life. If you lost all these material things, what would you do with your life? That's the important question.

Many survivors of deadly experiences do a 180 or even a 360 degree turn in their lives. They walk away from their jobs and homes and start living a life they want to live. They are positive and growing again. They don't go down a path of victimization, they become a strong survivor and see themselves as a different, better person. They have learned one important thing; you can't take it with you.

There are many paths in this life and many archetypal roles we can live and learn from and then live another one. Most of these roles are the lessons we came here to learn and then go on to the next one. The problem is most of us get stuck in the same role and think that's who we are.

Let's look at a couple of examples of my life so you can get the general idea. I started out as a victim when I was four years old and my step grandfather molested me. I didn't know it at the time but he was doing this to all the girls in the family, my sister and cousins as well. When I was nine, I stood up to this man and told him if he ever touched me again, I'd kill him. Back then I'm sure I meant it. He backed off and I didn't talk to him ever again. I learned what the victim role was early in life but decided I wasn't going to play it for very long. This experience made me strong at a very young age.

The next role I played was wife. I got married at 18 and really wasn't ready for it but I took it on anyway. Three months into the marriage, we received custody of my ex's two year old daughter. I became the mother role. Then three years later we had our son and my role became wife, mother and soon I had to take a job to help support the family.

The roles I took on all fit into the wife/mother category. I was the brownie leader, the club scout leader, the car-pool mom, the dinner maker, cleaner of the house, kisser of the skinned knees, and everything I thought a mom should be. I might have been trying to be an over-achiever as a mom because many times my ex wasn't at home. I felt that his love for alcohol was much more than his love for our family so I would take the kids and leave to go shopping just to get out of the house. I could've put myself in a victim role, feeling sorry for me and my children, but I didn't allow it. I had already learned that lesson from my childhood and I wasn't about to go back.

Finally when my son left, I kicked my ex out. Had I learned about being a victim; yes but I had also learned to put up boundaries in my life. The thing I hadn't learned was who I was. It seemed I had been following everyone else around on their path and cleaning up their messes, even my ex's. I was tired and wanted to find out who I was. I was 46 and thought it might be too late, but I was wrong. I went into the role of a strong woman. I was lucky because I could have walked into the "poor me" victim role at this point and complained about what had taken place in my life so far, but I didn't. I found I was stronger for the experiences and figured I had wasted enough of my life on everyone else and wanted more.

Now I had been in the "caretaker" role for a long time and old habits are hard to stop. I'm still working on it every day and remind myself to pick and choose who and what I want to take care of. This way I don't get "stuck" or get into the role too deep. It's fine to be a caretaker, but when it runs or ruins your life, stop it.

I met several men after my divorce and I started looking at the roles they were playing and it became fun. One was "a knight on a white horse" and wanted to save me and all the women he dated. It didn't work because I didn't need saving but many women out there do. They're in the "save me" roles. The problem is once they are saved, they usually end up being a victim to the "knight" because he wants them to do what he wants because he saved them. It can be a nasty circle.

A couple of the men were the "I'm the greatest thing you're ever met" role. These are the bigger and better than life men. These men are usually playing out some kind of fear about themselves and the world around them. They are very insecure men and have a hard time with a strong woman and will walk all over a weak women. (See I have learned something)

Some were victims and I recognized that right away because I had started out that way. As I grew as a person and started learning who I was, I could see more clearly who others were and what roles they were playing. I could spot someone who was in a role I had been in years ago. I look at some of the friends I had back then and see they are still in the same role and their life is miserable with little or no change.

Most of us start living our lives when our kids leave the nest. I, for one, couldn't wait until my kids moved on with their lives. I was a mother but I never really thought of myself as a mother type. I love them dearly but I'm not a clinging mother and never have been. I guess that type of role was not in my contract in this lifetime.

I have been in other relationships since my divorce and most of them didn't last longer than a few months. I was experiencing what I didn't want in a partner. Many of us stay in this "I don't want this relationship" for a long time. We fear leaving because of the unknown. We're afraid we might not make it on our own. We are afraid of really letting go and finding our true path.

My path is helping people empower themselves. I do that by my readings, teaching, coaching and writing. This is who I am, not just what I do. That's the big difference and with everyone I meet, I look for my lesson in it. This is my path and I love it. I'm always on the move, creating and recreating what I want in life. It took me awhile but I think I'm getting there.

I know who I am and it's great. Learning is a lifelong adventure and we never really get to the end of it. Even when we die, we learn on the other side. So take a look at what role you're playing and if you are ready to let go and move on to experience another one. It's fun to move from one to another once you understand these archetypes and know what they are.

There are several different types and they can branch off to fill whatever we "need" to experience in our lives. It's believed that archetypes are symbols or energetic imprints that exist in our psyches. They are usually understood by the language of the mind to help you trigger your memory of why you're here and the truth behind the illusions of reality. They can give us messages from our mind that verbal or written communication information can't.

Archetypes are a language of the mind with different frequencies of thought. There are individual archetypes as well as universal ones. They are a series of metaphors set into motion from any number of unconscious events such as tones, notes, meditation, out-of-body experiences and other means of conscious and unconscious communication and symbols.

The following is a list of character archetypes that we play out in our lives. It's fun to look at them and maybe identify yourself with what you have been and what you are now. Here's a short list of archetypes and just a brief disruption of what they mean.

The Scholar: The scholar is perhaps the most underestimated type of individual that exists in character building. He/she can be extremely calculating, highly intelligent, rational, an excellent strategist, and extraordinarily... vain.

The Soldier: Strong, willful, ready for a fight, whether it is for profit, or for revenge. May use sheer force to solve any problem. They seek to force their will on the world, directly or indirectly.

The Politician: Rather than facing conflict, he/she seems to beguile, distract, and utilize words to walk around it. Usually he/she is highly intelligent with strong social skills. He/she is specifically dominating, persuading, and/or manipulative.

The Priest: The priest is a visionary. He/she can see something that no one else can, and the faith he/she has in themselves, or something higher, he/she sees many things others can not. He/she can accomplish what seems like miracles.

Hero: Wants to save the world or anyone he/she thinks needs saving. He/she doesn't realize that not all people, animals or places want his/her help.

Mentor: there are different kinds of mentors but they are all teachers, leaders, learners and can be followers.

Shaman: Helps guide people on their own path, not his/hers.

Shape shifter: Many times misleads people by hiding his/her true intentions and loyalties.

Fool: Reminds us of our own follies and humanity and mirrors back how we might be acting diversely for our own good.

Shadow: Represent the energy of the dark side, the unrealized, unexpressed or unknown.

The Child: A pattern of hope and promise and may have trouble with a harsh world

Magician: Seeking balance for his/her personal karma

The Empress: The image of fertility, creator of life. She could be a mother who has a lot of children, whether they are hers or anyone else's.

The Hermit: Even in his/her isolation has learned and seen more than most of us.

The Wonderer: Always looking for self as if a barrier stands in his/her way of this mind, body and soul and the ability to bring them together as one.

The Judge: Represents law, justice, punishments and rewards. You can be the judge and still be working under the "devil" archetype.

The Devil: Adversary and strength both in positive and negative ways. Ego has a lot to do with how we play the devil role.

The Star: To twinkle and be seen and admired by all

The Knight in Armor: Trying to save the beautiful maiden, whether or not she wants to be saved.

The Maiden: Can be innocent or hide her ways behind a curtain of lies.

The Victim: Someone who is always looking on the negative side of things and can't move on.

Please remember that each of these can be played in a positive or a negative role. The choice is ours. We are the actors and directors of our lives. We decide how we want to play the role. There are many more archetypes but I wanted to list just a few so you would get an idea of how they might be working or not working in your life.

Also, we can be playing several of these roles at one time. We don't have to just be one or another. Humans think it is fun to combine and to play more than one character all the time. But really look at yourself or someone else closely before you put a label on them and remember, they might be labeling you too.

So finding our path is as easy as doing what we want to do; when we want to do it. Walking our path is as difficult as doing what we want to do when we want to do it. Walking our path isn't easy but it can be fun and an adventure if we view it right.

So instead of wondering where your path is, look down at your feet and take a step. Is the step straight ahead or is it to the left or the right? What direction do you want to go? Are you satisfied with your life now? If not, how can you change it? That's what our path is really all about. Change and how we play the roles we have come here to play. Change is the most important part of life. Nothing stays the same, nothing!

Instead of asking someone to help you find your path, ask for help in walking the path you have chosen to walk. The Help will tell you if you are on the right path or not. Believe me I know from experience.

Your path is really just one day at a time and how you live that day. That's our path. The choices we make, the words we speak, the thoughts we have and the way we treat others. That's us living our path, one day at a time. If you do this and become conscious of all these things, you soon look back at your life and find you have been walking your path all the time and the lessons along the way have been invaluable. This is the path of life and wisdom.

What we discover when we die

Death is a word that doesn't even come close to what happens to us when we go home and the physical body returns to the Earth. Death is a misunderstanding of life after life. I'd like to tell you what I feel we learn and where we go when we die. After all, I was there once.

When I had my near-death, out of body experience, I found myself in a very loving cloud of Light. I had no pain and was completely at ease watching paramedics trying to save my life. I knew my body was dying, yet I felt no anxiousness about it. I was just a spectator watching a scene in a play. I could hear everything they said and see everything they were doing. It was interesting but I wasn't attached to it.

I can remember thinking thoughts and questions and having the paramedics answer them like I was speaking to them. I remember the feeling of total love and joy and how I could have stayed in that cloud forever. What brought me back into my body was the sight of the chest paddles they were getting ready to use on me.

I remember thinking, "I don't want them to use those things on my body."

It was at this point when I became aware of a presence behind me. I had been so involved in watching the paramedics and what they were doing, I had forgotten to look around and actually "see" where I was.

I no sooner thought this when a voice from behind me said "Go back and stay conscious."

It was the most loving voice I had ever heard. I felt this wave of love that I have never felt on this side. I started to turn around to see who it was, but never made it. I slammed back into my body with an amazing force. I've never been the same since and I'm very grateful I'm not.

This experience brought me the gift of spirit and clairvoyance. It started me on the path I'm still on today. I wouldn't change it for anything. I think if everyone almost died and could remember it, we would cherish life more.

Death has been a mystery since life began. It will always be with us because anything made from or part of this universe has to end sometime. This is how it's supposed to be. Death has been talked about and recorded in every civilization since civilization began.

Let's look at death and see what we can understand about it. Religions have been telling us about death for thousands of years. They have been scaring the hell out of us because they want us to believe and be good. Well, I don't believe what most religions want us to believe.

Most of my information can't be proven because I'm getting it from the people who have crossed. I'm asking them to help fill in some of the myths and confirm the truths. They are as much a part of my life as the people are on this side of the veil. So here goes.

I think many of us are not afraid to die but are afraid no one will notice we died. I think we're afraid no one will remember us. Most of us aren't movie stars or "important" enough people to have our lives recorded and played back years after we are dead and gone. I, for one, feel lucky about that. I don't want my life analyzed and examined and questioned. I just want to live it, learn from it and then go home.

We should try to remember that dying is only a transition. Right now on Earth we're discovering many things about how energy works and many things aren't as they seem. We are uncovering mysteries of the past and learning things will be much different in the future because of these discoveries. And hopefully one day these discoveries will prove death is only a transition.

When I speak with souls on the other side, they tell me many different things. The one thing they all agree on is they've all gone back to about the age of 35 in our Earth years. This seems to be the metaphoric age of our soul. It's an age most of us relate too as far as usually being in good health and having a good time in life. I know even on this side of the veil, once we hit forty, most of us still feel 35 or so. Even my mom at the age of 83 says many times she feels 35.

What many souls tell me from the other side is amazing. They are healthy, young and are still creating and learning. Many have told me after their life review they want to come back again. We seem to have a lot more "guts" on the other side than we do here. I think that's because when we're in the energy body, we aren't attached to human "things" so we can see more clearly what life is all about.

Souls look back on their Earthly accumulation of "things" and laugh. They now understand these things aren't very important. They understand they were just borrowing them until they die.

Many of us hang on to "things" from our family members and friends who have crossed and that's fine. These things will help us remember these loved ones and the events we shared with them. These "things" are like the remembrances we hold in our energy body. We look at the "things" and remember. Many times we don't think about our loved ones until we look at something that reminds us of them.

Our loved ones on the other side don't want us to grieve for them. They don't want us to live for them or to think of them every minute of every day. They want us to go on with our lives and enjoy what time we have left in this lifetime. They see the importance of life and living each minute to its fullest. Grieving for them only takes valuable time and energy away from us.

On the other side, I see everyone connected, yet as individual as we are on this side. Their connection seems to be more of an energy and telepathic transfer. It's like we can take what we call energy on this side of the veil and use it for whatever we want on the other side. When we crawl into the human body, we don't see or feel this energy connection between each other and so we don't think we're connected at all. Humans want to see something to believe it.

Energy bodies, or what I call our souls, have no limits that I can see. They seem to be either light particles or dark particles. The dark particles appear as darkness to me when I see them. Like a dark cloud of rain in the sky but you can see through it. Light particles appear to me as a ball of light I can see through. I believe our souls are made up of these energy particles of either light or darkness, depending what we decide when we die. I believe free will never leaves us and our awareness continues even in death.

I don't pretend to understand this awareness. I just know when I was watching the paramedics work on my lifeless body from the white cloud I was floating in, I was still conscious and knew everything that was happening. I was functioning. I "felt" great. I knew where I was and can still feel and see it.

I also knew I was transferring messages through my thoughts to the paramedics because they were answering all my questions. I felt I was somehow communicating with them using telepathy. I know telepathy is still very much an unproven transfer of energy in the scientific community, however so are many other things we believe in or just take for granted. We don't have anything to measure this transfer of telepathic energy so it can't be proven beyond a reasonable doubt but neither can some other emotions we believe in.

The energy transfer of love, hate and other energy emotions can't be measured or proven yet we don't question them. We can prove how the cells of our bodies react and move energy through the food, water and air we take in to feed them because we can see them. However, we aren't advanced enough yet to prove what happens in the "unseen" world of energy. We can see and prove how energy is transferred from cell to cell and even within a cell to feed its self. We can "see" this because of our microscopes and other scientific equipment.

We have proven that every color, sound and object has its own individual vibration of energy to make it what it is, but yet we question telepathy. Telepathy is only a transfer of these vibrations to communicate information. For example; the vibration of the color red is telling us it's red. The word "red" is only a representation of what the vibration is telling us. But it does make you wonder why red is red and not blue. Is it the vibration of the color red transferring that information to our brain? When we hear the word red, why do we see the color and how do we know what shade of red something is?

We can't measure love or hate but we feel them and acknowledge that they exist. We can't see them except in our body's reactions, which isn't the measurement of the emotion but the reaction we have to the emotion.

Telepathy can't be measured but we can see the body react to it. We can't measure any of these energies but we can feel them and experience them. We believe in love and hate without being able to measure them but we don't believe in telepathy – that doesn't make sense to me. Both are only energy transfers from one body to the next. Both can have mental, physical or emotional reactions.

Many people argue that we can measure love and hate through cell reaction in our bodies and I agree with that. I also think we are just starting to learn more about the brain and the role it plays in these reactions. If we study it long enough, one day we might see the physical reaction to receiving telepathic messages. We aren't there yet because we are a very young species. Whales, dolphins and even sharks are showing us they communicate in many ways we don't see or understand. They have all been on Earth for millions of years. We have along way to go before we catch up with them and the understanding that communication is much more than the spoken word or even body language.

We're all connected because we're all part of the same Earth and species called Human. Just like dogs are all connected; no matter what "breed" they are, they're all dogs. Cats are cats. They all share some of the same DNA that makes up that species. Just because some humans are born in China and some in the United States doesn't mean they aren't connected in some way. They are all part of the human race and that makes them connected.

If we aren't connected in some way, how do different people in different countries come up with the same ideas at the same time? We're always connected to each other and the energy around us. If we can "prove" radio waves go on forever when we send them into space, why can't we understand our thoughts do the same thing? This can't be a double edged sword. If one thing works, then the other one has to work too. I don't think we can just believe in one energy transfer because we can "prove" it and throw out the rest of the theories. We are an undeveloped species that can't prove a lot of things yet.

Souls on the other side don't have bodies like we do. They don't have a brain, taste buds, hands, eyeballs or any of the other organs we use in this dimension. If they don't have all these organs, how do they communicate? They do it through energy. Thoughts are energy, just like radio waves. Radio waves are energy. The souls on the other side use this energy to communicate.

When I communicate with souls on the other side, I get a message in my head. I relay that information to the person who has asked me to do the reading or get in touch with the "dead" person. I tell the person what I'm hearing and it's amazing the accuracy of the information. If I've never met the person who asked for the reading and I've never met the person who is supposed to be dead, how do I know these things? Where's the information coming from?

Some say I'm reading the mind of the person sitting in front of me. Well, if I am, that would prove telepathy because they would have to be thinking about this information at the time for me to get it.

Some people say if I am reading their mind, I'm not communicating with a "dead" person or soul at all. If I wasn't communicating with a soul, how can I tell the person in front of me what the "dead" person did before they knew them? Sometimes things come out that only the dead person knows or that their mother or siblings know and I have to wait to hear back to get a validation.

Science can't prove this but this is my world. This is energy transfer from another dimension in the form of either telepathy or something we can't prove or don't understand yet. But isn't that why we're here; to learn?

Energy is probably the biggest part of our lives and yet we take it for granted because we don't fully understand it. It can be used in so many ways to make our lives better if we just thought about it more and what it can do for us. Too many of us walk through life not understanding energy and the way it works. We don't understand that for every movement and thought, energy is flowing and bringing to us the reaction to our movement or thought. It's so simple but we make it hard.

When we're on the other side, that's all we use. We use energy for everything. We know its secrets and it becomes fun and enjoyable. On the other side, we talk to each other though energy. We renew our life force by absorbing more energy. We build things with energy and we communicate with others through energy. On this side, it's harder for us to materialize because we are in a different dimension.

Many ghost hunters think ghosts have to draw on the energy in a room to get enough energy to materialize into a form we can see. I'm not sure this is true. Because we are pure energy on the other side, we don't need more energy. We need a different kind of energy. What we have to do is match the energy in a certain place. We need to lower our vibration to match the vibration of the place where we want to materialize. We pull on the energy to match its vibration so materialization can manifest itself in this dimension. A change in dimensions has to mean a change in vibrational current of some kind.

My scientific friend has reminded me that there have been numerous studies but nothing has been proven about why ghosts materialize sometimes and then don't in others. There is no way to prove or disprove my theory. It just makes sense to me. If we go to a different dimension when we leave this one, then we have to change our vibration. We have a higher vibration because we are pure energy and the human body cannot support pure energy without exploding. You have to join this dimension and become part of it to be visible by the human eye. That's my theory and I'm sticking to it. If it's wrong, so be it.

What's hard to understand are the images we see that aren't really souls, just implanted energy. Implanted energy is where someone or something has been for a long time and probably died there and left an imprint of their human energy. It's not a soul that comes back to haunt the place. It's like playing a video tape over and over again and there is no communication or interaction with the image you see. There is no soul or life there, it's just energy doing the same task over and over again. If it were an actual soul, it would look at you or make a noise or something. Remember there are several different ways a "haunting", as we call it, can take place and not all of them have a life force behind them.

Souls soon learn trying to stay attached to the physical world when they aren't physical just isn't possible. Sometimes this can be the cause of what we call a haunting. They just want to be back on Earth but can only be in this dimension for a very short time. They don't have a body in this dimension anymore so they don't have elements of this dimension to help keep them here. This is when we might catch a glimpse of someone but they can't stay too long without a physical body.

They can watch and learn and make noises so we know our loved ones are around but this isn't a haunting as much as they're trying to let us know they're around us. They don't want to come back to the physical world to live, they're just checking in to see what everyone is doing. That's the big difference between a haunting and a soul who's just looking in on us.

When you ask a vision to make noise or they seem to be trying to communicate with you in some way, there is a soul behind it. When you see a cloud of darkness out of the corner of your eye, it can be the presence of a dark entity or just dark energy. Demons are usually dark energies we have created over the thousands of years of believing in them. Remember if we can manifest good, then we can manifest evil too.

We need to be aware of the many ways energies that are at work on Earth and in space. We don't understand many of them because they work differently in different dimensions. Until we can safely travel between dimensions with our human body and human brain, we'll just have to guess at how some things work.

There have been times when I've been in another dimension with my energy body and I've seen strange things. It doesn't last long and I feel I'm not in my body when it happens. My human body is too heavy and I have to leave the body to raise my vibration to go to the next dimension. The fact remains that I can't stay there very long because my human body calls me back. As long as my human body is functioning, I'll have a connection to it.

Even if I was in a coma, there would be a connection. I wouldn't be in the body but I would be around and checking in to see if I could go back or if the body was going to die.

Sometimes the body is so badly injured, we can't go back.

When we die, we learn what this life is all about. We get a life review and see what we did and didn't do. There is no judgment about it and we aren't punished, we just learn.

A few years ago I asked the Universe to show me what some of my past lives had been. I was sitting quietly in meditation with my eyes closed when suddenly there seemed to be a black and white movie playing very quickly on my eye lids. I saw I had been a servant and was stabbed to death. I was a priest and had been poisoned. I was a witch and was hung in my own front yard. I was on an island and my jealous lover pushed me into the ocean from a very high cliff. These are all some of the lives I was shown and how I died.

The deaths didn't bother me. It was like watching a movie of someone else. It was very informative and I really learned a lot about myself during the 2 minutes or so I was being shown all these lives. I never saw myself as a queen or king or anyone very special, but that's okay. Not all of us can be royalty. Some of us have to be just plan, ordinary people. And after all, my lives were planned by me on the other side before I came here so I guess I never wanted to be rich and famous.

That's another thing we learn when we die. We learn we have the free will to plan another life here on Earth if we want too. Not all of us want to come back; however, many of us want to come back again and again. The time frame of when we come back is up to us too. We can come back the next day or in 1000 years.

Many of us decide to stay and rest and even study on the other side. I know there are times I'm sitting in my front room and I can look around the room and see faces on the wall just looking at me. I have asked what these souls are doing and the answer I received was they are just watching and learning.

Many of these souls are "seeing" what is going on in the world right now and deciding if they want to come back. Coming back is not just "I think I'll return" and you come back. We have contracts we make with lessons we want to learn or experiences we want to experience.

We can choose any number of lessons we want to learn and we need to pick our parents. This usually happens even before our parents are born. Sometimes these things are written and agreed on hundreds of Earth years before we are born so the lineage of our family continues in a certain way to learn certain things. You may have agreed to have certain parents but that also means you are picking your grandparents and all the relatives that go along with that family in that time period.

This can take thousands of years, but all we have is time. When you live forever, a few thousands years are nothing. We can also decide to come back to the same family very quickly. There are several cases were a grandparent died and came back in the body of a baby that their granddaughter was having. Of course, this was also planned long before it happened. We can chart lessons in one lifetime that will help us in the next one, whether we come back right away or stay on the other side for a billion years.

When we incarnate, the lessons we put in our contracts are activated. We start right from day one with our learning process and our dying process too. We walk through this life and every day we learn a lesson in some way even if we don't recognize it on a conscious level. We have the choice to learn these lessons the easy way or the hard way. We also have the choice not to learn them at all. We can go in a different direction and learn something else.

There is no harm in this other than we'll probably have to come back at some point to learn the original lessons we wanted to learn. Our parents and all the relatives and friends and people we agreed to meet and interact will help, but they all have free will too. This means our parents might get here and decide not to birth us into the world. If this happens, our contract is put on hold until we can arrange to have someone else birth us that will give us the same lessons.

It can get very complicated but I think this has been going on for so long, we don't think anything of it. It's just the process we go through, just like the process of life on this side. On the other side, we're busy planning, learning and growing as souls. We don't just sit around on a cloud all day long wondering what to do. We are watching over loved ones who are still on Earth and trying to help them as well as learning things we need to learn in case we want to come back.

Souls on the other side can travel at the speed of light because that's really what they are, so they can get to many different places in the blink of an eye. A lot of this is hard for our human brain to understand and I don't think we supposed to understand it all. If we understood why we're here, we wouldn't have any fun trying to figure it out. There'd be no point in us being here or coming back. We're here to learn so we shouldn't know everything before we get here. It just wouldn't make sense.

We also learn when we die just how old we really are. We have been around since the beginning of time and I don't mean in just this universe. When we die, we see we're billions and trillions of years old. We get to see all the things we have experienced in this lifetime.

When we cross, we understand we continue on no matter what we did or didn't do here on Earth. This is "Earth, a learning school" just like the next universe we move onto will be a different learning experience. Each universe has a lot to offer and we have a lot to learn.

When we die we look at everything differently. The only thing that means much to us is what we learned. We do care about our loved ones back on Earth but we understand they have to continue on and learn what they came here to learn. We understand we were part of a contract and now the contract has ended for us and we can start planning our next role.

Imagine you're the actor in a play on this side of the veil, and when you die; you get to see the whole play, not just the part you were playing. When you're playing this part, you get so wrapped up in it sometimes you forget to look at the whole play. Dying is just stepping off the stage to see what is really happing to our soul. Dying is a rebirth on the other side.

When we die, we disconnect from the physical and see what we really are, spiritual beings having a human experience. This is life and this is death. This is why I hate the word death. It should be said we are just changing from one world, the physical world, to another world, the energy world. This makes more sense to me than death. When we "die" we learn we aren't dead at all.

I've done several readings where the people on the other side were surprised at where they were. They didn't think there was a heaven and they find they aren't really in heaven but feel like they are home. Some people don't go into the light and want to stay attached to Earth. This is free will. They can stay here and try to be attached but it will never work for them. When your vibration is not matching the dimension you want to live in, you can't live there. Something has to change. You either need to find another human body to live in or move on into the light. Staying in this "not physical but not a Light being either" dimension is hard on your soul.

When we die, we don't die – only our Earthly body dies. We return to where we came from and we continue to learn and grow and do things. Many people on the other side show me they are reading and creating new things. Because we are all connected, we can help each other create and travel in groups if we want to. Here again, the human brain is very limited on what it can comprehend or make sense of. We just need to remember, not everything makes sense in this world. It doesn't make sense because we haven't explored it enough or found the answer to it yet.

Learning, growing and creating is all we know and all we do. Look at what you create every day. Life is just an endless series of choices and movements. We create something every time we make a choice or even move. Death is the same. We have choices and we create out of energy.

People on the other side show me they can create a house out of energy. They can travel into outer space and come back in a heartbeat. They aren't dead by any means of the word; they're just in a different dimension. They don't have a human brain so they don't think like humans anymore. There is no ego, hate or jealousy. Those are all human conditions.

I've also never run into the "devil" in my line of work. I have run into negative energy or souls who don't want to go into the Light so they stay in a dark place, but never the devil. I also don't believe in the devil. I think our egos are the devils and make us do things that get us into trouble or we regret later. When we start to listen to an out of balance ego, trouble can start.

Freud believed that we start out with an id – which is an identity. This is when we are babies and this id doesn't care about anything but that we are taken care of and get what we want when we want it. We don't care about other people or their feelings. At about 3 years of age, the second part of the personality starts to develop. Freud called this the Ego. He based the ego on the reality principle. The ego understands other people's needs and desires. It understands that being impulsive or selfish may hurt us in the long run. The basic job of the ego is to take care of the id while being considerate of the reality in any situation.

About the age of five, the superego develops. This is the moral part of us and its development is affected by our caregivers or parents and the moral and/or ethical restraints placed on us as we grow. The superego might equate to the consciousness as it really dictates our beliefs in right and wrong.

According to Freud, in a healthy, balanced person the ego is the strongest part. It can satisfy the needs of the id yet not upset the superego, while taking into consideration the reality of every situation. However, if the id gets too strong, impulses and self gratification takes over and the person becomes selfish. If the superego is too strong, the person could have rigid morals and be judgmental and unbending in their interactions with the world.

So if our ego, or id or superego is out of balance we can be out of balance with our reality and morals. This can create havoc in our physical world as well as affecting us in our spiritual and energy world. It can make us selfish, radical and unbending to anything but what we want and what we think is right. This could lead us to live in hell here on Earth.

Every year I do thousands of readings to talk to souls on the other side and I've never run into one that's in hell or is hanging around with the devil. I would think if there was a devil, he would have shown up somewhere in these readings and either told me to leave his souls alone or threatened me in some way. I really think the devil is an out of control id, ego or superego and it gives us someone else to blame instead of taking responsibility for our actions and thoughts. We create our own individual devil.

We know this is a duality universe so if there's a heaven, there has to be a hell to balance it. Well, there is no heaven or hell. There are only dimensional changes and energy. Some people call Earth hell and that would make outer space heaven. Souls that don't want go into the Light when they die don't go to hell. They stay in a dimension where it's hard to manifest and hard to do things. This would be a hell. They haven't gone into the Light so they can't become Light beings but they aren't human either. They're in a half dimension I think. (I know it can't be proven unless quantum physics will do this at a later date.)

We're in the third dimension. When we die we can go into the fourth, fifth or sixth dimension because we have let the light of energy come into our energy body and fill it completely. However, dark souls might be in the third and one-half dimension. This half of a dimension is something we think isn't possible but I think it is. If we don't fill with light, we are filled with darkness, but we aren't in the third dimension because we don't have a body either. The body has died its third dimensional death, we haven't.

This is how I believe souls get stuck in a dark or gray area. They don't want to go into the light for any number of reasons but they can't go back into their body so they are stuck. This is why some of them actually try to get into our bodies when we aren't looking, so to speak.

When we're on drugs or alcohol and we've let our defenses down, many of these dark souls will enter our body. The saying, "Man, he isn't himself when he drinks" has more truth to it than most people think. Our soul can't live in a body where the vibration is off because of drugs or alcohol; it leaves and waits for the body to clear itself of the harmful substances. As the body works to get rid of these poisons, the vibration changes and at some point the soul can re-enter the body.

If a dark soul has been in our body, we'll feel it when we are sober again. We feel off, our energy is low and it can take hours, days or even weeks to feel "right" again. We need to understand there are energies who would love to take over our body so they don't have to go into the Light and be reborn. These souls don't want to start over the hard way. They want to just pop in and keep going. If a dark soul enters your body when you're on drugs or alcohol, it tries to keep you out so it can stay in the body. Remember dark souls aren't in the Light but aren't physical either, so they can match your substance abuse vibration better.

Some people think there is a judgment when we die. I think this is because religion has put this fear of "judgment" on us for so long. There is no judgment, just a review and then we decide if we want to come back again or not. Even murderers can go into the Light and see the harm they did. There is no judgment because every soul knows there will be karma to pay. That is one of the rules we can't change in this universe. So even if people don't seem to get their karma back right away, it will come back to them.

I had a friend once that got herself into a lot of trouble because she hadn't paid taxes and wasn't playing by life's rules. She tried to kill herself on more than one occasion but just couldn't seem to succeed at it. I told her that karma's a bitch. Instead of dying, she had to live and face her problems. She was getting her karma back in a way many of us don't understand. Her karma was life and taking responsibility instead of dying and going home to rest. So there doesn't need to be any judgment because we can't get away from this law of the universe. Karma will always come back to us, always.

For those of you that haven't heard of karma, it's an ancient Sanskrit word. The Aryan people spoke this now extinct language before 3000 BC. It means causation; cause and effect. Causation is the "causal" relationship between conduct and result. So karma is believed to be the result of a past action and the intention of that action. This proves that even thousands of years ago there were people on Earth that believed in "what you put out, you get back".

Simply put – if you put out negative energy, you will get negative energy back. If you judge someone, you will be judged. This is the way the unseen energy of the universe works. We can't prove it, but we can see it in our lives if we really stop and look at events that happen to us. Karma is just another one of the rules of the universe that we can't prove but can see the end result.

Karma can work for us or against us. If we are trying to do good and help others, we can receive good karma and good things. However, even the Aryan people believed the intention behind the action or thought was just as important as the action. So if you are doing something good just to get something good back, that's as bad as doing bad to someone. We should be doing good because it feels right and it helps someone and not because we want something good back.

This is where karma can be a bitch and bring us things we never wanted or expected. So I would really watch your thoughts, actions and the intention behind them. Because like the Aryan people who believed in karma thousands of years before Christ, there just might be something to it – whether science can prove it or not.

There are all kinds of things we learn when we die. We see the "one with the most toys doesn't always win." Toys are just that, things to play with for awhile and then we have to leave them behind. We enjoy them here because we are in the human body and we have adrenaline that can rush through our veins and give us a feeling of joy and danger.

We don't have danger on the other side. We know we can't fall off a cloud and hurt ourselves. We know even if we go to another solar system, we can't get hurt in our energy body. Our soul doesn't have blood and adrenaline. It's just energy. It might sound boring but we can do many other things when we're dead that we can't do here. Remember we go from one dimension to another. Each dimension has its own creative force and "toys" to play with.

I do believe we are supposed to be like children at play in each dimension. I think we'll understand that when we die. I think the dimensions of time and space are so great that our little human brain can't even begin to understand them. I also think we aren't supposed to understand them. We are supposed to learn from them and have fun. I believe we truly are like little gods experiencing him or her self and taking that experience back into the collective consciousness of spirit. We learn all of these things when we die and look back on our lives. This is probably one of the reasons we want to keep coming back.

Death is not the enemy, nor is it the savior. Death is a very important part of life. Death is a new beginning. Death is a way of cleaning and clearing our soul from Earthly attachments that are really our illusions of life. Death is a way to clear past and present karma. Death is a way to experience rebirth. Death is what we make it. It can be welcomed with love and light as just another part of life or we can view it as negative and dark. The choice is always ours.

When we die we learn so much about what we were doing on Earth in the first place. All questions are answered because we no longer have the false illusion of Earthly life to cloud our vision of what's real. We are the only "real" thing in this universe, galaxy, solar system, and as far as space stretches. We, as souls, are the only thing that'll last forever and ever. Even if you don't believe in a higher power, there is still something inside telling you this is the truth of life.

I've talked to a lot of souls who were surprised because they really thought there was nothing when we died. When they walked into the Light, they found they were home and there were so many others they could talk to and learn from. This is what we find when we go home.

If you watch the dying, most are not worried about it. Many talk to people we can't see before they pass. Many look at the ceiling and smile at something unseen in our dimension. They hear things we can't. They get this wonderful peaceful look on their faces and there seems to be a peace that surrounds them. This is the knowing of our soul that home is just a heartbeat away.

Being an animal communicator has helped me to understand death from the animal kingdoms' point of view. Animals know all about death. They know they have to be aware of what is happening around them every second because it could mean death to them. All animals, even domesticated animals, have this built in survival DNA and knowing. Even humans have it; we just don't recognize it like the animals do.

When an animal is weak or ill, they look for death to take them home. They don't want to suffer. They want to die and go home to rest. They may even go out and look for a predator to kill them quickly.

Here's what I've learned talking with animals about death. First, they can jump out of their bodies very quickly and then back in if they want to. When a predator jumps on its' prey, the soul usually jumps out of the body and is home before the body is dead. If you really look into an animal's eyes as it is being attacked, they go blank. This blankness is also in the eyes of humans that are close to death. This is the soul leaving the body. Without the soul, the body has no real life to it. The heart can continue to beat but it's just a muscle that's doing what it was meant to do, nothing more.

Life is the soul. The body can function without a soul as far as the heart beating, the blood pumping and muscles twitching; however, it can't walk around consciously knowing what it is doing. It's like a chicken with its head cut off. The body still has blood pumping and until all the blood is pumped out, the body will do what it's supposed to do. The body may run around because of the adrenaline in the muscles but there is no life in the body at that time.

Death is a condition, just like life is. Don't judge it. We can learn a lot about life when we die. The other side is not about sitting around playing harps and being bored. It's about living in another dimension and experiencing things in that dimension. It's about always living no matter where you are. It's about learning forever and creating forever. Death is just another adventure and when we die, we are free again.

We leave behind this heavy body and all the things that go with it. We fly high and we are free to do what we want. Death is only a rebirth on the other side and our friends and loved ones meet us and we understand what we were doing on the Earth in the first place. What a great way to end a life – going home.

Remember to talk to the dead and do it wherever and whenever you want. They don't stay in a graveyard or in just one place. They travel and move and create and do things. They visit us and encourage us and love us like they were still in this dimension. Talk to them, they can hear you. When I was out of my body in my near death experience, I could hear everything that was happening.

Remember they aren't dead; they're just in another dimension. It's like looking in a mirror. We can't go into the mirror but that doesn't make our image any less real. Death is like that. Live, learn, love and die. That's the order of things in this universe and until we actually become "god", we can't change it. Maybe it's different in another universe but this one is a school about life, learning, loving and dying. It's a specialized school and the lessons stay the same. All we can do is decide how we are going to learn them and move through them.

Bible Stories, Fairy Tales, Horror Stories, Fables, Legends and Myths – What's the difference.

It seems no matter where you look, every civilization has had its own stories of life and death, what it means and how to live "right". Many of these stories parallel each other and all of them have some kind of moral, lesson, or hidden warning. Many of these stories have been modified or changed throughout time to match the time period in which they are being read.

Most stories have some kind of truth to them, even if it's a very small portion of the whole story. It could be as small as the country or the period of time in history the event took place. The rest could be made up just to get our attention.

Many believe the story of Atlantis is only a story because the city hasn't been discovered. Well the ark, with supposedly all its' unearthly powers, hasn't been seen or proven either, but that doesn't stop millions from believing in it. I think it's fun to sit back and watch what people believe in and what they don't, and the basis for that belief. I'm pretty open to just about anything that resonates with me but it has to make some kind of sense. It doesn't have to be explained, but there has to some kind of order to it.

Let's look at the story of Adam and Eve. It doesn't make sense to me because we have already proven there were other humans on Earth about the time the Bible says God made the first man and the first woman. And it doesn't make sense that if Adam and Eve were the only people on Earth and they only had two sons, where did Cain find his wife after he killed Abel?

Stories have to make some kind of sense. The story of Adam and Eve seems to be a fairy tale of how God laid out His plan of life and the contract he made with man. It told us that eating of the fruit of the Tree of Life was sinful without the wisdom of how to use it. This story tell us Adam and Eve ate the fruit and tried to hide their sin with fig leaves.

If you really look at the rest of the Bible, most of the Old Testament is telling us why this loving, powerful God is punishing all of mankind for the actions of Adam and Eve. This doesn't make sense to me. An all loving God sees two people screw up and we are all punished for thousands of years.

This is something only man could make up to scare everyone into thinking something was wrong with them from birth. Just because two people did something God told them not too, I don't believe all of us are born in sin. I don't believe we carry the "sins" of our fathers. We may carry the consequences of the decisions and choices of our fathers and forefathers, but that isn't sin.

Now, being an animal communicator, I've talked to a lot of snakes but not one of them has ever told me to eat from the tree of life and I think apples are getting a bad rap here too. I feel the tree of life is the knowledge we actually hold in our soul. Eve opened up to this knowledge but didn't have the wisdom or experience to know how to use it. After all, she and Adam were supposed to be two innocent humans that didn't know anything without God telling them about it. Could this also be the part of the story that tells us we are supposed to be like children every day and see the world in wonder and learn about it?

The knowledge part of the story reminds me of us. We come to Earth with all the knowledge of our soul, but because we have a human brain, we forget the wisdom or how to apply our past life experiences to use it. We wander around on Earth for years trying to figure out what we're doing. This story points out that we have all the wisdom and knowledge if we just remember it.

The nakedness of the couple signifies their openness and innocence when they first came to Earth. I think our nakedness as babies is still a representation of our innocence and we are NOT born into sin. If we were born into sin, I would think we would be born with a full suit of armor. When Adam and Eve put the fig leafs on, it represented another way of saying we are going to hide and lie to our mate and everyone else. These are the sins we do on an individual level. There's a saying that goes like this - "it's not if a human will lie, but when and how big the lie will be".

The story goes on about Adam and Eve having two sons. I think the children had to be boys for two reasons. First, back in that time period sons where more important than daughters. Second, the end of the story has a murder in it and people didn't want to think a brother and sister or two sisters could kill each other. (I wonder if it also gives credence to the fact that too much testosterone can get anyone into trouble, even with his brother.)

Almost all stories have a villain and a victim and there has to be a reason for an action to take place. The reason behind the Cain and Abel story was jealousy and competition. Of course, like in most fables, the victim was good to the core and innocent of any wrong doing. (Don't you think that all innocent victims should run around naked so the rest of us would know who they are and that they have nothing to hide?)

The warning part of the story tells everyone that even brothers don't always get along. It's a warning that even brothers will kill each other over material things or belief systems. It warns us that if brothers can kill each other, we can kill anyone. You see, we are all brothers and sisters because we are all connected with our human DNA.

Another part of the moral is to let others live their lives and you focus on you and how you want to live your life. It includes the fact that we are all individuals and different and it's okay. It also reminds us that we have to pay for our deeds, whether they are good or bad.

After the murder of Abel, Cain tries to hide the body from his parents, but God has already seen what he's done. Boy, I bet God had had it with this family already. Eve picking the forbidden fruit and then Cain murdering his brother could have been the last straw. God could have wiped them off the face of the Earth, but he didn't. There's another lesson here too. The lesson is about a parent's love of their children.

The hiding of Abel's body and the shame Cain felt because he had the wisdom and knowledge in his soul to know this act was not a wise one. He knew somewhere deep inside he would have to pay for this crime. The karma he created didn't kill him and neither did God. However the writer of the story said God put a curse on him and his children just like God put a curse on Eve, which was a woman's monthly period, and I believe both are untrue.

In Eve's case, the human body has to have an egg of some kind to form another human. This egg holds a lot of DNA that tells the new human who they are. The blood is the liquid of life, thus the two need to go hand in hand. It could have been a man who carried the child but that's not the way masculine and feminine energy works on Earth.

Masculine energy is the giver of an idea. The side of us that thinks up things, that gives the energy of manifestation to make things real. The feminine side is our nurturing side which takes the idea from the masculine and gives it time to mature and come into manifestation in the right way. So this is why women have "the curse" and responsibility of birthing. The feminine energy is one of nurturing. It has nothing to do with being a good mother.

(Just a note here - the two energies we carry in us have to do with creation and giving and taking of an idea to manifest that idea into reality. They don't have anything to do with whether we are a good or bad mother or a macho man or not. They are about us being balanced to create things in our lives.)

I think a man came up with the idea of a curse because they think a period is not a good thing. Some women have cramps and other uncomfortable symptoms that many men see as a curse. However, I don't believe it's a curse from God. I think this is how we had to birth new souls to Earth from the very beginning.

Why would God, if he's our Father, according to the Bible, hurt us and curse us? If he is this all powerful, loving God in one sentence and a judgmental hard ass in the next sentence, that would make him out of balance and maybe even bi-polar.

The story shows us the love that parents have for their children no matter what they do. This is a metaphor for the love the Bible tells us God has for us, if you believe in God. Does this mean if you don't believe in God you can't have this love?

If we can step back from the Adam and Eve story, we'll see several lessons and one of them is "what we put out, we get back." If you put out pain, anger, jealousy, lies, and hide from the truth, you will get back the same thing. It also tells us that someone somewhere will always see our actions – which can be thoughts or physical deeds. We can't hide from them. This is what most of the stories around the world have in common.

Many of the Bible stories are no better than some of our horror stories today about people killing each other over greed. They might not be as bloody or graphic as the ones we have today, but it's still a horror story of someone killing someone else over jealousy and trying to hide it from others. It seems us humans just love stories like this.

Look at all the fairy tales we have about wolves eating little girls in red capes that come to visit grandma. What a perfect horror story to tell your children to get them to hate wolves! We want children to love the world, yet we tell them stories like this when they are too young to really understand them and the moral behind them. What are we thinking?

Don't get me wrong, I think we need some of these stories to get our lessons and morals in a way that will shock us into them, but we shouldn't take them as pure truth. There are just too many things in the Bible and other religious writings that were written by humans, that science is beginning to prove didn't really happen. On the other hand, there are too many things that did happen that we ignore. Remember, life is actually stranger than any fiction someone could write about.

In almost all the stories that have been handed down through time, there is a villain, a hero and/or heroine, a victim, a conflict, and a solution. This is really life as we live it today. These stories have been around so long that we think we have to live them, but we don't. We can live a life free of being a victim or having conflict, and we don't have to feel bad if we aren't heroes and heroines.

Horror stories are big with people. People love to be scared to death. I'm not sure why that is, except that the adrenalin rush feels good to many people. Many of the horror stories of today show a lot of blood and very violent scenes that can be very upsetting to our sub-conscious and our consciousness. Our sub-conscious can take in hundreds and even thousands of pieces of information every second. If any of this information is repeated over and over again, our sub-conscious starts playing it back to us.

It's like a commercial to get you to buy something. The more times you see it, the more you want the object. The most common problem that arises from this is that we think the object is better than it really is.

We start believing in the commercial, which is one part truth and three parts selling mumble-jumble. We get so caught up in what someone else is telling us, we forget to really look at the product or object. We buy it because it has been almost beaten into our heads that it's something wonderful and when we get it, it's not at all what we expected.

I've talked to murderers, and even hunters of animals, and they usually say the same thing about the killing - they never expected it to feel or look like it did. The movies or video games don't have the emotions attached to the action they are showing us. The only way to get the emotion is to do the actual act and then it's too late. Then the emotions come to the surface and we have to face what we did.

When we read or do an action over and over again, we start to believe in it. We think it's the truth or the way things really are. This kind of "putting the old blinders on" can cloud our judgment of what is really true. We also have to remember that no two people will see life in the same way or believe the exact same way. We might agree on some things but because we all have individual brains that think differently with the lessons we came here to learn and because of our different up-bringing as children, we never think the exact same way. Even two brothers who were raised by the same parents can see life in different ways – hence Cain and Abel.

The Bible has been around a long time and many people think there is no other truth about God and what happened on Earth at that certain time. Nothing could be farther from the truth in my eyes. There were all kinds of different civilizations on Earth at that time and each one of them had, and still has, their own Gods and belief systems. Science is proving there were many different situations happening on Earth, in different areas, at the same time. To help people cope with these situations and experiences, they needed to believe in something bigger than themselves. As situations changed, so did their belief systems.

We are slowly starting to understand that nothing stays the same. Times change, beliefs change with discoveries, people change, the world changes – this is what it's supposed to do. We are also starting to understand that stories change with whoever is telling them. The story can go on for a long time and someone can add their own version, or it can be shortened and a lot of stuff left out. It's up to the storyteller.

Also, most stories are not told at the time they are happening. Some of the Bible stories were written hundreds of years after the event. Many times there was no one around who even knew if what the storyteller was writing was the truth of what really happened. So how could people know what really happened?

I really think many of the Bible stories, fairy tales, fables and the rest of the stories we hear about were made up stories like the stories we make up today about Freddy Kruger or Jason in the horror movies. A thousand years from now someone will probably read what happened in these fictional stories and think we were horrible people. They could see us as people who loved bloodshed just like those who threw people to the lions just to watch them be eaten. Are we really any better than that now?

I think the old devil stories are like our modern horror stories of crazed murderers in ski masks or people that can kill you in a dream. Because we still live with so much rape, killing, starvation, wars, torture, and mistreatment of people all over the world, we have to come up with something worse than what we live in to be afraid of it. We are so used to the idea that someone could break into our home and kill us, we have to come up with something worse to get people to be good; thus the invention of Hell. *(We humans are so creative it's scary.)*

Hell had to be something that would really scare the pants off people in the past and us today. For that reason, Hell was created as a place you could never get out of once you went there. The devil would hold you in terror, pain and torture the rest of your days; your soul would be lost forever and ever. There's a good bed time story if I ever heard one.

The people in the past understood the pain of torture and killing, the same as we do. They could visualize and even feel what it would be like to spend the rest of their lives in Hell, just like we do. What a horrible fear this is to think we have to live this hell here on Earth and if we aren't good, we live it when we die too. That thought would scare me more than Freddy Kruger and any nightmare on Elm Street. I'm glad it's just a story and not really true.

When it comes to stories about the devil, I always insert the human ego where the devils name appears, and then the story seems to make sense. The devil is another means for us to escape our responsibility. We need to understand we create and manifest our own devils and demons. So before you go putting more energy into the devil and hell, think about it. If there is no heaven, only a transition, there can be no hell. If there is only above and below, there is only space and Earth. Back before the need to control people, there was never a mention of the devil or hell. It was all good.

The stories that scare us the most are the ones we seem to hang on too. We seem to like living in fear and I'm not sure why. It's so much nicer to live in joy and happiness. We fear everything, and the Bible, fairy tales, myths, legends and horror stories feed this fear. We feed the fear of a powerful, forgiving but "send you to hell" God – which doesn't make one bit of sense to me, in so many ways. We feed the fear of the dark and what goes bump in the night. We feed the fear of murder and lies and corruption. We fear failure and we fear success. We need to stop all this fear.

We're finally starting to write new children's books to give them encouragement instead of scaring the hell out of them just before they go to sleep. The fairy tales of old may have some good lessons in them, but just like the Bible and other religious material, we have to change with the times. Situations don't stay the same. The only thing that stays the same is that we are souls having a human experience. That should be enough of a horror story for us to read and live.

If we read fairy tales of old to our kids, we should explain the true meaning of them and give our children the lessons behind the stories. We can really do that without a story too. We can do that by example and by living our lives so they can see and experience what life and living is all about. There are enough real horror stories out there for them to view and learn about, we don't need some wolf eating little pigs because they didn't build the right kind of house.

A three year old is not going to understand the moral of the story is hard work and dedication in any job will pay off. This is the moral behind the story, because the first two pigs were building their houses but wanted to take time out for relaxation and got eaten. Is this also teaching our children they can't relax in this life? This fairy tale was written in a time when people needed to understand the fact that doing things the right way was more important than doing them half-assed. This is the whole moral to the story. However, our children may only see a big bad wolf eating some poor little pigs that just wanted to have fun. This could give anyone nightmares.

I think this is why so many people have nightmares about the devil and demons coming to get them. We have put so much fear into the devil and demons in the last 200,000 years, it's implanted around us. We have to start changing that energy so we can get out of the fear. It's possible but it will take some time and it takes the majority of the human race to do it. It sounds impossible but it's not, it's going to take one person at a time believing it.

Some of the fairy tales show us that we are followers and when we follow someone instead of finding our own truth, we can get ourselves into trouble. Look at the store of Henny Penny and the sky that was falling. When Henny Penny was hit on the head by something in the barnyard, she thought the sky was falling. She wanted to warn everyone. She didn't take the time to discover what had hit her on the head before she panicked. So in her haste, she ran off to tell the king and try to save everyone.

Along the way she ran into several other animals. She told a cock, a duck, a goose, a turkey and then a fox. All the birds she met went along with her, and they all got caught up in the same fear of the sky falling on them. They all wanted to tell someone but only Henny Penny had actually experienced anything. She was the only one that had felt something hit her on the head, yet the others believed her story.

They were in such a panic that they weren't listening to their guidance or instinct, just their fear. The fox convinced them that a short cut to the king was through his cave. Well, if these bird brains would have been thinking instead of being in such fear of nothing, they would have never gone into the cave. Their instincts would have told them they were heading for danger. Nothing had hit them on the head like it did to Henny Penny, but they believed the story because of the fear they saw in the little chicken. They entered the cave and were of course eaten by the fox and his family.

The moral of the story is to pick your friends well and don't get in a panic over nothing. Check out what is happening around you before you make a big deal of it or "lose your head", so to speak. It's a great moral but a three year old isn't going to get it unless you explain it to him or her. It's a better story for kids in their teens but by then they don't listen anyway. A three year old will just see that the fox is a murderer and killed all these wonderful little birds. Is this a fairy tale or horror story? You be the judge.

Most belief systems want everyone to see their point, which is a good thing. However, when it comes to having a belief system forced on someone, we should draw the line. Seeing a point of view or belief is a lot different than being told, "If you don't believe that way you'll go to hell". That's just nuts in my book.

Many religions want us to believe in something other than our selves. I know there's a higher power that started all of this and keeps it all going. I also believe this higher power gave us free will so that we would have control over ourselves and wouldn't need to be controlled. Unfortunately, many people think they can put their free will on others and that's when the trouble starts. We are in control of our own lives, not a church or a "you're going to hell" religious scare tactic.

The story about Jesus going out into the wilderness for 40 days and being tempted by the devil is a great story of ego and learning to control it to become "christed."

"The Christ" was and still is a spirit that anyone can have. Back in the time of Jesus, there were things you could do to get this title and one of them was to go out and find your demons, so to speak. I equate it to the twelve step program of learning to stay sober, that we have today – metaphorically of course. I know that sounds funny, but if you make it through the 12 steps of sobriety today, you change your life and become responsible for your actions.

The rules were somewhat harder, like going out into the desert or turning water into wine but the basic outcome was the same. It made a person feel good about themselves, take responsibility and help others through their devils and demons.

If a person made it through all the requirements in the old days, they were considered a Christ. So Jesus did all the things on the list and that's why he was considered a "Christ". He wasn't the only one with this title. I'm now wondering if the story of Jesus was more about becoming a "christed soul" than anything else.

This story really shows there was no devil, only the ego. After all, Jesus was only human, just like us; and just like us, he was a child of God or a higher power. According to the trinity, Jesus was God, man, and Spirit, so if he was part of the Higher Power that made him, Adam and Eve and us are part of that power which makes us no better or worse than Jesus. If you use this analogy, we are God, man and Spirit too.

They called Jesus, the Christ, but back in his day, this was a very common word for someone who had completed a list of tests. These tests were to show their faith in God. Even today anyone can live with a "christed spirit" because it's an energy not a person or place. This Christed spirit is available to all of us.

This brings up the story of the Ten Commandments. Wow, that one will blow your mind. Meeting God on a hill in the form of a burning bush – I thought only the devil had brimstone and fire around him. I have to say that all my visions of a higher power have been very loving and comforting, not scary or overbearing; so go figure.

Anyway, the Ten Commandments are supposed to be the word of God to live by and many of them are great but some are not realistic. I've listed them below with my opinion of them.

1. Thou shalt have no other gods before me

   I think this was a real attempt to get people to believe in one religion and have only a few people in charge. By the time this "rule" came to be, there had already been thousands of civilizations who had never heard of this "one god". And what "one god" is there anyway? No one's ever really seen him or her. Most people who think they have seen God describe a bright light, not a person. So how do we know what god is right? If we all just understood that no matter what we call this higher power, it's all the same and there is no real difference from one god to another.

2. Thou shalt not make unto thee any graven images

   Humans are very visual and need something physical to see and feel so we can believe in it. And just look at all the statues and "graven images" we have today that sit around on our shelves to remind us we should be good and believe in one god. So what would a picture of Jesus be considered? Humans will believe anything if it's put into their sub-conscious long enough. Look at what Hitler did. Maybe people needed these stories of healing and being saved back in the time of Jesus. Also, many of the stories of Jesus were written 700 years after his death. How would we know if the stories were right? No one was still alive to validate them.

3. Thou shalt not take the name of the Lord thy God in vain

   I don't like cursing either but I don't think God really cares about it. He's too busy to care about our language. He looks at our heart and soul. This one always meant that you believed in one God and never said a bad thing about him to anyone. This rule was taken way too far and many people were killed in the "name of God". I don't think a loving god would have wanted this. I often wonder if this God just shakes his head when he looks at what we become when we enter the human body.

4. Remember the Sabbath day to keep it holy

   I feel this is another attempt at control because when God made the Earth, who's to say what day he rested on. There were no weeks or days back then, only sun up and sun down. We should hold everyday holy, as it means we are still alive and can have more fun in the human body. It doesn't matter what day of the week it is. Man made weeks and named the days, not God. I'm sure he could care less. Also, on the other side of veil, there is no time, space, days, weeks or years. That is all a made-up human way of keeping time and bringing some kind of order to our lives.

5. Honor thy father and thy mother

   That's a great one but in this present day and time there are some parents that don't deserve honoring. I'm sure there were some undeserving parents back then too. Is this another way to take control of us at a very young age? If you didn't honor your parents, you would go to hell. There's a bedtime story for the young ones.

6. Thou shalt not kill

   I agree – goes along with Cain and Abel. But this is just common sense and if you believe in karma, you don't want to do this anyway. You know it will come back to you.

7. Thou shalt not commit adultery

   Many believe this includes even sexual thoughts when you look at someone else. Let's get real about this. Sex and sexuality has been around since the beginning of time and will probably always be in this universe. All species have physical reactions to outside stimuli that can't be helped. It's the pushing of these feelings or sexual actions on others that's not right. This one should really say, "do not commit rape".

8. Thou shalt not steal

   I agree but, here again, we are talking common sense and karma. I wonder if the priests of that time even listened to these laws because they were the worst offenders, just like many politicians are today.

9. Thou shalt not bear false witness against thy neighbor

   This is "thou shalt not lie but let your neighbor live their own life as long as they aren't hurting or harassing you". In other words, live and let live. Another common sense rule, which many of us don't have.

10. Thou shalt not covet

    Many believe this means not to want your neighbor's husband or wife in a sexual way; however, it can mean not to want anything anyone else has. In other words, work and get it yourself. This is one I agree with too. We have too many people who think this world owes them something. Mother Earth owes us nothing. We are the ones coming here to learn and grow, and we can't do this as long as we are letting someone else make our choices or we are so wrapped up in "wanting" something that we can't see the true meaning of life. In other words, get over it.

In my opinion, about half of the Ten Commandments are control and half are common sense and really have to do with karma. The story behind it is funny. Moses was supposed to come off the mountain with the Ten Commandment stones for the people that were waiting for him. He was very angry because they had become bored and built an image of a golden ox. They were worshiping it and dancing around it. Can you just imagine his anger because God had just written, "Thou shalt not make unto thee any graven images". I'll bet Moses was more than just a little angry and so his temper must have been right on the edge.

One story tells us that when he threw the tablets at the people and they broke into a thousand pieces and were destroyed. So if Moses was this mad at the people for worshiping the golden ox, how did he remember what God had written, word for word, on the tablets he had just destroyed? I know I wouldn't have. I would have had to make something up later. I guess that's why I'm not a saint yet.

Don't get me wrong, I think some of the Ten Commandments are good, but they are common sense and how we should think anyway. But we are human and most people don't have the common sense that would fill a thimble. They live by ego alone. That's why we have to keep coming back.

Most stories have to have someone or something tangible or visual for us humans to be able to believe in it. I think this is why the Bible stories, the fairy tales, myths and legends have lasted so long. There are other stories of where we came from and how we got here but because they say we come from another dimension, we can't wrap our brains around it. Even many of the Greek gods seem more real to me because the stories say many came to Earth and took humans as their mates.

The Greeks had many gods and believed that anything was possible. One of their stories is about Pan. Pan was a man who's lower half was a goat and the upper half was a man. It's rumored he was the son of a god and goddess but not everyone is convinced of that. Some say he was the offspring of a human mating with a goat or sheep. Some say he was good, while others say he was evil.

Some say he was only a myth to be a lesson to mankind to keep to his own species and leave animals to their own species. Some say he was the last of his kind. Some say he was a shape shifter that got stuck in an animal's body. Whatever Pan was or where he came from, he disappeared as quickly as he appeared. Myth, lesson or truth, you be the judge.

However, the stories of the Universe and the powers we can't see are the ones that seem to die the quickest. It seems if we can't see it or experience it, it doesn't exist. Yet all the other stories that science is proving wrong still keep going on and on. Many times we think if it was good enough for our parents, it's still good enough for us. Well, that's right and wrong. Today is a different time from yesterday or even ten years ago. We have to keep things current because they won't work in the past or in the future. They have to work for us right now.

There are so many stories, that not all of them could fit into one book. If you did get them in one book, you wouldn't be able to carry it around. That's why I'm only giving a few examples here. You pick your favorite stories or legends and see what you get. Stories are part of every culture around the world.

Every civilization has its' stories of gods, goddesses, saints, heroes and victims. The Aborigines have a great way to look at life and death. They have been on Earth for over 50,000 years and they have great knowledge that has been passed down from one generation to the other without a book or any written word.

The Aborigines believe their elders are like the voice of God. They represent the God of a particular area and have been given laws for that area. They call it "dreaming". The laws are actually how the society is run. "Dreaming" is like the Bible to Christianity or the Koran to Islam. It's where their authority comes from and where their ceremonies come from. It's everything to them and the elders pass it along to the community.

Aborigines believe that when someone dies, they go back to the Spirit World. They become what they call "ancestors". They become spirit guides for the living however their name is never mentioned again and no one else can ever be named that name. This is done out of respect for the family. They also believe that God doesn't hide behind a blue sky or stars. Their understanding of him is that he is here on Earth. He is in a waterfall or in trees, river or lakes. This is where God lives and these things are his home and we are his children.

The Aborigine people have been around for a long time and yet they have ruled themselves with "dreaming". They are among only a handful of civilizations that have existed that long. The Romans came and went as did the Atlantians, the Mu, people on Easter Island, the Mayans, Incas and tribes from every part of Earth. Most of them disappeared because they got greedy and/or the leaders were too controlling, mean, war-loving and hateful. They really destroyed themselves.

History will repeat itself until we get the lesson. Just like situations in our lives will repeat themselves until we get it. The event or situation may appear or be brought to us in different ways, but the lesson will be the same until we understand it and do something about it. We should take a lesson from the aborigine people and live by the laws of the land and honor everything we have today and the people around us. That's what life is all about.

So really look at the stories of today and the stories of the past. What resonates with you and what doesn't? What makes sense and what doesn't? Start questioning stories, myths and legends. Start looking at what part of them might be the true part and what part might be someone's ego. Look at the lesson in them. Are they something put out there for control and fear? If they are, get rid of them.

We have enough fear in us from the past to last another 10 generations. We should be the generation to put a stop to that fear. Some of us are living a horror story - stop it and look at how you can change it. If someone you loved died, stop and know they aren't dead; they're just in a different dimension. I feel and talk to my dad on the other side all the time. Humans want to see and feel things to believe they are real. Stop and see the signs your loved one is sending you from the other side and feel the energy when they are near.

The stories of near death experiences and people who have visited the other side, like I did, are some of the most real stories we have, yet we pooh-pooh them. These are the stories we should be listening to. These are stories to show us there is life after death. These stories are more real than a horror story of aliens coming to destroy us. These are the stories we should be listening to so we can understand what life is really all about.

Like I said in the beginning, there is always some kind of truth or lesson in any story. It's up to the individual that is reading the story to figure out what that meaning is for him. Henny Penny might mean something different to everyone that reads it and some people may not get the hidden meaning at all. They may just think chickens are dumb animals that don't seem to reason things out.

Many people see the devil as something scary and fearful, yet there are stories about a god that turns people into salt because they looked back at a burning city. Wow, who should we be afraid of? I think we shouldn't fear either. We should fear our own ego, thoughts and deeds.

So have fun with the stories us humans put out there. Remember there is some kind of truth or lesson in them. Find out what the story teller is trying to tell you. Then move through it and don't let it run or ruin your life. Life is just another story that you'll tell others when you die and return home. Life is as simple or hard as we want to make it. Make it simple and believe in common sense, karma, and the rules of the universal energies and let all the other dogma go. Don't let someone else tell you what you should believe or why. Look at the stories and see if they make sense to you. If they don't, let them go; then write your own story with your own truths in it.

This is just a note to remind us that most stories, legends and myths arose out of many non-literate societies in which they were passed down by word of mouth. This wisdom and knowledge was spoken and repeated for thousands of years. There could have been errors and the stories might have been changed due to different thought patterns of the story teller and the changing times.

It's only when we see written language, not word of mouth about events that happened in the past, that we can say we have scientific records that can possibly be proven. Science looks at the spoken word or stories as just words in the wind and with no "written record" it can't be proved it ever happened. But that's not to say written words are always the truth, as proven with even the fiction we write today.

We need to understand that some of these "written" stories, which we take as the truth, were written hundreds of years after an event, so they might be just like the spoken stories, nothing more than words in the wind that have been changed and embellished over time.

Spirituality vs. Religion

I often wonder what's wrong with humans. Many of us believe in things that aren't real and don't believe in the things that are real. The "wanting" to believe in something is a powerful force in humans. We feel this overwhelming "need" to belong to something, someone or some place. I believe we have this feeling because when we're in the human body, we don't see the lines of energy that connect us. We see the energy lines on the other side and we know we're connected. When we incarnate into the human body, we forget. We are all part of a larger whole. We forget we are connected because we are all part of the human race and human consciousness.

We feel if we don't belong or aren't connected to some kind of belief system, club or organization, we think we're missing something. We think there's something we need to find or have or do or fulfill. We don't see that belonging to something made of this Earth or in this dimension will soon leave us or we'll leave it. Nothing we own while here on Earth is forever, except the soul we carry around that brings life to our body.

The people we live with or meet in our lives are there for a reason but we don't own them. The things we have in our lives are there for a reason but we are only borrowing them until we leave this dimension. The places in our lives will go away with the changes of the Earth and we won't have them any more. This is the way of life.

This may sound depressing on one hand but look at it on the other hand. It's change, and it's growth; it's seeing that nothing's as important as our life and becoming our own best friend. We don't need anything else. All the "other stuff" we have in our life is just the icing on the cake, so to speak, and we just enjoy it.

Many religions tell you that you need something in your life besides you. Spirituality says the most important thing in your life is you.

Let me see if I can explain this. I believe we are already part of a higher power, no matter if you call it God, Goddess, Buddha, Mohammad or whatever you want to call it. So if we're born with part of a higher power already inside of us, we don't have to go looking for it. If it's already in us, like the DNA from our parents, all we have to do is go inside ourselves to find it. This is getting to know ourselves from the inside out.

If we would do this instead of looking on the outside to find something to make us complete, we would already know we are complete without needing anything from the outside world. We would take care of ourselves first, knowing that if we aren't healthy or in a good space, we can't possibly help someone else get healthy or happy. This is another difference between spirituality and religion; knowing you are already part of a higher power and you don't have to do anything or except anyone into your life to prove it.

Religion tells us we have to "find God" and be saved because we were born in sin. I don't believe that. That's like telling our children they are bad right from the start when they haven't even taken their first breath. This is a teaching of old that was put in place to scare people and make them think something is wrong with them right from the birth.

It doesn't make sense to me. If God made everything and it was good, why would he make us and tell us we are bad from the beginning? And if he made us, wouldn't we be good too? This relates back to the fable of Adam and Eve and making us think we did something wrong from the start. I just can't wrap my head around sin to begin with.

Sin is supposed to be something we do wrong and are punished for it. Sin can be anything in religion. It can be as big as going against the Ten Commandments or as small as not believing how a religion tells us we need to believe. It can be cheating on your husband or wife or even being gay. Sin is something man-made and is therefore not important to me.

I believe we are here to learn and we will make mistakes while we're learning. This isn't sin, this is living. If we do something that is a violation of someone else's spirit, there is a law set up in the Universe to take care of that violation. It's called karma. So don't worry about people who seem to get away with everything - karma does and will come back to them. It might be in a different life but their karma will have to be dealt with eventually.

I don't believe in sins. I believe in learning lessons. We can learn them the easy way or the hard way. This is what we are here to do - experience and learn. Sin is another way of saying "if you don't behave, you'll go to hell", and of course I don't believe in hell, or heaven for that matter. There is only a transition when we die. We are only going from one dimension to another.

Another big difference between spirituality and religion is that religion is man-made. It's a controlling organization no matter what label it has. All organizations have rules and laws - that's why they are called organizations. Organization means to organize and you can't have organization without rules, at least not in human terms.

Most religions tell us where we should worship, what we should worship, when we should worship and how we should worship. Spirituality says, live your life with love and respect and you can't go wrong. Spiritually says worship yourself and how you are living your life.

Religion tells us we are "God's" children and then makes us feel if we don't "mind him" we'll go to hell. Religion tells us to be kind to one another, yet if someone doesn't have the same belief system, they are looked down on or judged as wrong. They are seen as "sinners".

Spirituality says there is no hell. There is only the karma you create in your life and you have to take responsibility for it and your actions. You can't blame anything on God, the devil or anyone else. It's all up to you and what you do.

Religion is really good at making people feel guilty or wrong; after all, religion has been doing this for thousands of years now. The problem is religion isn't changing, however, people are.

True spirituality is an ever changing way of thinking and believing. Spirituality changes with what we learn about ourselves and how we want to live our life. It grows with us and we expand with it. It should always feed you and make you eager to learn more about life and death. It should challenge you to think on your own instead of telling you what you should think or believe. It should feed you and make you feel good. Not condemn you and make you feel guilty.

We all want to belong to something. Instead of belonging to something that controls you, belong to something that frees you. Belong to yourself, not others. I had a friend that was taken in by some people who were acting like they were spiritual people but they weren't. They were actually cult leaders. It almost ruined not only her life but that of her husband and kids. Luckily, they all got out and away in a very short time.

Remember, spirituality and religion can both be used in love or in fear. There are both sides to every organization. There is good and bad in both religion and spirituality. That's the duality of this universe.

I've written down about 10 items to help you see if you are dealing with religion, true spirituality, or cults. It's not all of them but they are my favorite top 10. *(Remember, I'm not saying religion is bad or spirituality is better, they're just different. Many religions are starting to come around to being more open about things and realizing as we prove more and more about what happened in the past, the Bible might not be the history book so many have thought it to be.)*

1. Cults will try to tell you what is right and wrong and how to live your life. Control and fear are the tools of this organization. They spread fear, guilt and mistrust and make us question ourselves and others. There are some religions that do the same thing. If any religion or belief system tells you this, run as fast as you can. This is just control and power. Spirituality says the only control you need to have is control over yourself.

2. If someone acts "holier than thou", run because they are not coming from the true spiritual side of anything. They are operating from the place of ego and control. Some of us are smarter than others and some of us do better at life because we play by the laws and rules of the Universe, but we are all in this together and should never look down on anyone. Spirit says to look at each other with love and then let it go.

3. Guilt, fear and disconnecting you from friends and families are tools cults and some religions use to take control of a person. True spirituality is living a life surrounded by friends and family, no matter what their beliefs are.

4. True spirituality is change. It changes with our way of thinking with new discoveries, and new times. It's says we were wrong about the past and that's okay. We believed what we thought was right at the time and now we know different and it's good. Most religions or cults won't go this far.

5. Most cults and religions don't recognize our inner strength without "belonging" to something. They don't see humans as their own individual god who is creating their own world, just like God created Earth. Spirituality recognizes the god within you. It's looking on the inside for strength and listening to your own inner voice so you know what's best for you.

6. Most religions want you to come to their church and pray. Spirituality is "a knowing" that a Higher Power is listening to you whether you are in a church, a car, on a hillside or in your own room.

7. Many religions collect money for God – God doesn't need money. It may go to support a building or a cause but it's not going to God. Many religions want money more than they want to help people. Spirituality tells us that the Universe will provide us with what we need if we ask. Money is only another form of energy and it comes and goes.

8. Spirituality says that prayers and positive energy are just as important, and maybe more important, than money. Bet you'll never hear that from a cult leader without some kind of threat attached to it.

9. Many cults and some religions will pit family members against each other, using this as a way of control. They will also shun family members that don't follow their rules. This causes a lot of grief, fighting and mistrust in families. True spirituality would never do this.

10. Many cults and religions put the fear of God into people by telling them the devil is in them or that he will take them to hell. Most spiritual people don't believe in the devil or hell. They understand we create these dark energies ourselves. So if we create them, we can destroy them.

The difference between religion and spirituality is religion pushes itself on you where spirituality says live how you want; it's your life and your responsibility.

More people have been killed in the name of a religion and the belief in a "certain" god than for any other reason in history. Religion tries to hold us in fear and damnation. It tells us we were born in sin and we just can't seem to get away from that sin no matter what we do, unless we believe what "they" want us to believe. True spirituality says live how you want to, believe what you want to and let others do the same.

Religions and other belief systems have been ruling, running and ruining our lives for thousands of years. The "fear" of god has been bred into us for a long time. Luckily, we are now entering a time when this fear is falling away. Religion isn't serving people anymore. There have been so many stories of child abuse, mental and emotional abuse, and control in churches lately that people are wondering what is happening to religion.

Well, this is the way religion has been for thousands of years. There have been abuses and atrocities going on for so long, it's stupid. Many religious leaders have been taking advantage of the writings of the past and putting their own spin on them for way too long. They interpret these writings to benefit themselves and not the people. This happens in organizations and clubs too, and even in governments. Whenever a new leader comes into power, everything has to change.

If we really step back from all the organizations, clubs, cults, religions, and any other organized gathering of people, we'll see the same patterns that come into play. There has to be a leader and they almost always want things run their way. It's not about what happens just in religion, it's about what happens to people!

Before "man-made religion" there was a worship of Mother Earth and all that was on Earth to enjoy and cherish. People saw God in everything. They felt the power of life and energy in everything and in all places. These people were the first humans on Earth, but as with all of us that enter a body, we change.

There is something about being in the human body that makes us go nuts. There is something about the brain not being able to comprehend the true meaning of life that gets us into trouble. We don't see our connections so we get defensive and greedy. We live in a fear of everything and many belief systems just add to this fear.

True spirituality does not control anyone or anything. True enlightened people can look at another person and allow them to walk their path without comment or control. I volunteer at a penitentiary and work with many men who have committed murder, rape or robbery. People ask me how I can even talk to these men. My answer is, "I don't know their lessons or their path. I don't judge them for their past mistakes. I look at what they're doing today to better themselves."

True spirituality is playing by both the laws of the Universe and the laws of the land. This is one lesson even Jesus taught. Whether you believe in him or not, one of the most obvious points he was trying to get across to people was this, "Pay the taxes and live by the man-made laws, but don't lose the fact that no one can control your thoughts or your heart."

The story about Jesus talking to John the Baptist when John was in prison is a great lesson on how powerful our brain is. Jesus told him to look into his heart and mind and know he was free even though the bars of man kept him imprisoned. He was telling John that most of our suffering is created in our own minds.

This is one reason history states the Jews hated Jesus. They thought he had come to set them free of the taxes but he didn't. Jesus realized that money wasn't the important factor, it was your life and the way you thought about life that was important. He was trying to tell the people to start freeing themselves by changing their way of thinking.

This story's meaning is still the same today because we still have taxes, laws, and other people running governments that just don't get it. Real power is in your thoughts and in your heart, but not in money. You can have all the money in the world and still be lonely, unhappy and wonder why you're here.

I've come to realize that money is just another form of energy. It comes and it goes, and if you manage it well, you will always have some. It's like your body energy or your brain energy; if you do too much physical activity without getting your rest, you are soon tired. If you think too much without giving your brain a rest, you become mentally tired. The key to having money is a give and take, just like every other form of energy in your life.

Another myth that religion likes to spread is you have to go to church to be heard or accepted by God. I think this relates back to the days of old when the belief was that only a priest could talk to God. People had to pay priests to pray for them. If they couldn't afford it, they went to hell. I think this belief system is still in play in some areas of religion throughout the world, especially if you look at the TV evangelists.

I believe in giving and sharing but I know God doesn't want our money. I know many preachers and healers that don't charge and let people give what they can. They have faith that the universe will take care of them.

Just because "man" wrote in the Bible that God said to tithe, is not proof to me it always means money. It can mean other things. Money is a man-made commodity and God could care less about it. Humans are the ones that have given money so much power that it now rules us. It's everything to us and it runs and ruins our lives.

Money could be the "carved images" that the second commandment talks about. It states that no other "god" should come before "God" and we should not bow down nor serve this "carved" image. Isn't that we are doing with money at the present time.

Could it be that in our guilt of worshiping a "carved image", (which is money); we think if we give it back to God, we'll be forgiven. See how much the past teachings of religion and its laws and rules have affected and infected us about money.

I don't believe God wants your money. He wants you to learn who you are and what you want in this lifetime. He wants you to find the answers to why are you here. What do you want? These are the important things. Money should only be another means of energy to get you where you want to go.

Talking to God can mean talking to the trees, the water, the sky or whatever you think the higher power is in your life. You can do this anytime, anywhere and it costs nothing.

As I'm writing this book, studies are showing that religion has stopped growing and more people are starting to believe in themselves and in science. People are starting to believe they need to move forward with some kind of action to take control of their life instead of waiting for God or someone else to do it for them.

This goes right along with the saying, "God helps those that help themselves." In spirituality we call this action and showing the Universe what you want. If you start doing things that will bring you closer to the future you want, the universe will see it and can then supply the means for you to get it. However, you actually have to make some kind of effort to get it. You can think all you want about something, but until you take the action to manifest it into reality, not a lot will happen.

I believe if you start to go in a certain direction and things aren't working out, it's only the Universe telling you to look at it and see if you are going in the right direction. It doesn't mean God is against you. It means to look and to see if you are doing it right or if something else might be better for you. The Universe knows your contract and will do everything in its power to steer you in the right direction without taking your free will away.

Many religions will steer you in their direction and tell you how to believe. All organizations and clubs have rules to follow. The Universe also has rules and laws to follow, but they are designed to help us succeed and grow into strong souls. If we learn to work with these laws and rules, they can work for us and not against us. Most of us see a rule and want to break it, instead of letting it work in our favor. If we would just stop resisting what we can't change and start working with what we can change, our lives would be better and easier.

There are a couple of laws that rule the Universe that we can't change. The main rule to remember is "what we put out, we get back". The other rule is our thoughts, words and actions are always based on some kind of intent. We either intend to help someone, hurt someone or ignore someone. Look at your intend very carefully before you do or say anything.

The laws and rules of the Universe deal with our thoughts and actions and come with the punishment or reward of karma. Many religions don't teach or understand karma. In spirituality, karma is the law to live by. It's the law of taking responsibility for your thoughts and actions. Many people will use excuses like, "God told me to do it" or "the devil made me do it" or "I did it because the church told me to".

These are sad excuses for our actions. It's been my experience that if a person does something for any of the above reasons, and breaks the law or hurts someone, then the church, cult or organization is not going to stand behind them and take any part of the blame.

However, this is where karma comes in. Karma is a great energy and law of the Universe. I've seen and heard people in church gossiping about other people and then wonder why someone is talking about them. That's karma!

Some people use the church as a social outlet and there's nothing wrong with that but many of them leave their good social behavior behind in the church as they walk out the door. Don't get me wrong, there are also some very spiritual people who talk the talk but don't walk the walk either. I've had my share of "spiritual people" who want to run the show and tell everyone it has to be done their way or it's not the right way.

It's the same with any of us. We can talk about what we believe but do we really do what we believe. Most of us are so influenced by our outside world and what other people will think, we don't follow our true beliefs; we follow everyone else so we can fit in.

Ever watch groups of people? There is usually a leader and they want the attention of the others. They seem to have more knowledge or wisdom; whether they do or not is another question. They are looked up to or, in some cases, they demand the attention and respect. Many of them do this with fear and control.

Then a new person comes into the group who seems to have the same amount of wisdom and the leader feels threatened. The leader goes into a panic. We now have competition.

Competition can turn anyone into a controlling, angry person. We feel we have to be better, wiser or stronger than everyone else. This is our ego working in overtime. Our ego wants us to prove something to someone even if it's wrong.

When we get to a point in our lives that we can invite anyone into a group in hopes they can teach us something new or we can learn from them, we have moved past the resistance that keeps us stuck. When we have moved past competition, fear and panic, we have moved into a knowing of self and being okay with ourselves.

Many churches won't allow me to come and talk because they don't believe in reincarnation, life after death, animals having souls, or even my clairvoyant abilities, and that's okay. What they don't understand is that I'm usually the first one to tell people, "None of us know it all but keep your mind open to new things and see what resonates with you." Don't get stuck in the ways of the past that are eating you. Be open for the present ways of feeding you.

There should be no competition when it comes to learning about yourself and others, or our souls. We should embrace the saying, "When the student is ready, the teacher appears and when the teacher is ready, the student appears." Whoever is supposed to come to us for business, counseling, readings, advice or whatever, is supposed to come to us for a reason. It's as simple as that.

Religion and spirituality can be the same in many ways. Maybe I need to clarify it by saying, people, whether they're religious or spiritual, can be judgmental and/or nasty, and controlling or good and caring. It really depends on the person and how they want to use their power.

Religion and spirituality can change our lives for the good or the bad depending on what we are being told to believe. I've seen people live a horrible life because they think they are sinners and have to suffer. I've seen people get confused because they are told God is great and good and to fear him. How can that be? I've seen spiritual people tell others that to be spiritual you have to meditate and do certain exercises. Nothing is farther from the truth. It's all doing what you feel is right for you and your belief system.

Let me tell you my experiences with churches. When I was about 6 or 8 years old, I went to church with my grandparents. My grandmother, my dad's mom, was a very religious, born again Christian. My grandfather was her second husband and no blood relation to me or my family. He was a "holier-than-thou" type of guy and the pedophile I talked about earlier. I used to hate to have them say grace at a family dinner because the prayer was so long the food was usually cold before they were finished.

They went a to a holy-roller church and wanted me to go with them. I had no idea what it was like at this church. My only experiences at that time with going to church had been the calm and quiet Baptist church my parents sometimes took us to.

The church was big and there were hundreds of people there. The music was nice but when the minister got up to preach, I thought all hell had broken loose.

He was yelling and screaming and I was scared. Then everyone started jumping up and yelling and I wanted to run out of the building. I didn't understand what was happening and it did put the fear of God or something in me. I only wanted out!

It was a crazy experience and one I've never forgotten. I never went back.

My parents had taken us to a Baptist church when I was very young and I can remember the kids' Sunday school and then going upstairs to the main sanctuary for the Sunday service with the grown-ups. The thing I remember most about these Sundays was going home and having Sunday dinner. The sermon didn't stay with me but the roast, mashed potatoes, gravy, carrots and homemade dinner rolls filled me for hours. That was the best thing about Sundays.

I went to a Nazarene church in junior high for awhile, but only because there was a boy there I liked. I don't remember much about it except the youth group was fun because we went skating and did other activities. I once attended a Catholic service and knew right away it wasn't for me. Then it was on to a Protestant church for a couple of Sundays. After I got married, I stopped going all together. The only time I was in a church was for a wedding or a funeral.

It wasn't until I was in my forties, and after my near death experience, I found a church that was close to my beliefs and to what was happening in my life. It was a church of psychics, healers and other spiritual people. It was a place to study my clairvoyance and open up to the new path I was beginning to walk. It was great, up to a point; then came the rules. It seems most humans have to have rules because they just can't figure it out for themselves.

This church was different from many other churches because most people were psychic and we studied the Universe and its energies. We did readings on people and we worked with chakras and meditation. We worked with positive thinking and manifesting physical things through thought.

I was moving very fast into my psychic life but the church rules said you had to go slow and do readings their way. I began to get bored and wanted to learn faster and move quicker. *(I'm told this has to do with the fact that I'm an Aries.)* I soon felt the church was holding me back and left.

The year I was there was great, but I had my own rules and my own life and that was that. I knew all the rules just weren't right for me. I still speak at a couple of churches around where I live but they are spiritual and allow me to talk about my belief system. Their way of thinking is very close to mine but I still don't go to church on a regular basis. I feel I'm my own church and I can talk to a higher power any time I want to without going into a building to do it.

I have watched and listened to a lot of people and it seems many of them go to church just for the social time, not the message. They want to look good in the community. In many cases, church can become a social status. There's nothing wrong with this but if it's just a social club, so to speak, the church service probably won't be very meaningful to you. You might as well join a gym.

However, religion and spirituality do have their place in society. It's when either of them gets so one-sided or radical they become destructive that's just not good. There is a good side and a bad side to everything. This is the way our universe works.

When either religion or spirituality becomes a "you must live the way I tell you to live", it becomes bad. Both religion and spirituality should allow people to believe their own truth. Both agree there is a higher power running the show but many think "their god isn't or can't be the same as someone else's god". That just doesn't make sense to me.

The ancient Greeks, Mayans, Druids and many other civilizations had several gods they prayed and spoke to. Many of these cultures thought there was a different god or goddess in everything. There was a sun god, a night god, a harvest god, a water god and the list goes on and on. They believed a god or goddess was in everything on Earth and they tried to honor everything, except other human beings.

I think it's strange we can see God or a Higher Power in everything but each other. We don't want to kill or harm God's creatures, but we will kill each other in a second. More people have died in a name of a "god" than for any other reason and it's really stupid. I don't think any loving god would want us to kill someone else in his name. That's nuts! I believe it's ego and fear in humans that's telling them they need to get rid of someone they fear.

This goes for both religion and spirituality. Neither is perfect, nor will they ever be. They are both part of the human consciousness and that is about as imperfect as it gets.

The dark side of both beliefs conjures up the devil, demons and sends dark, evil energy out into the world and sometimes onto other people. All this darkness can be used to control, scare, run and ruin people's lives. Because the dark side of things seem more mysterious and forbidding, more people are either afraid of it or feel more powerful if they are in it. They feel they are breaking the rules and therefore are more powerful. If they could see they are only creating dark karma for themselves, they would soon stop what they are doing.

Both religion and spirituality are very powerful systems because people want and need something to believe in. People are trying to fill a void of loneliness that they have on the inside by looking for it on the outside of themselves every day. They will never find it on the outside. Charlatans of both religion and spirituality know this and it's when people are at the lowest point in their lives, these charlatans make their move. They see the fear in a person and feed off the self doubt and wanting to "belong" that a lonely or unhappy person might be feeling. They tell them they can somehow save them or make their life whole, happy and complete again. Nothing could be farther from the truth.

We are the only ones that make ourselves whole or happy, but humans are very much "pack" animals and need to belong to something. They feel lonely or unwanted if they don't. So when someone comes along with a promise that we can be part of their group, many people jump at the chance before they look at the whole situation.

Once they're in, they find out it's not what they wanted at all. They learn they have to do what someone else tells them to do. If they do it, they will belong and everyone will respect them and love them; if they don't, they will be kicked out. This makes the person feel even more unloved and unlovable. They think something has to be wrong with them because no one wants them around. This is a gang mentality too.

Cults of all kinds do this to people. What people find in many cases is after they are in these "loving organizations", they have to hurt others, or if they break a rule by thinking about what they really want, they are punished or damned to hell. These organizations take away "free will" and free thought. If you find this is happening to you or someone you know, run or get help from someone who understands the cult system.

I look at life this way - you have to walk your own path. You have to learn your own lessons and you have to do what is right for you. You can't walk a path that isn't yours without being unhappy or feeling something isn't right. You can't walk a path if it's not yours to walk. Life is a learning experience and living it is the only way we learn.

I can't walk the same path my best friend walks even if we think close to the same way. I'm not her and she's not me. No one is like you and you aren't like anyone else. Our thoughts, beliefs, opinions and actions are ours alone. This equates to, you can't be wrong and you can't be right, you just are. You are just who you are and you are what you think you are.

Both religion and spirituality have their power symbols too. Religions have crosses, Rosaries, the Star of David, snakes, goats, and so many more I can't name them all here. Each religion seems to have its own power symbol that somehow makes people more powerful if they use it or pray to it or believe in it.

Spirituality has at least as many symbols if not more. They have crosses, crystals and other stones, the yen and yang, the labyrinth, Taro cards and this list goes on and on too.

I think Edgar Cayce summed it up in one of his readings. The following is not a quote but is close to what he said.

You can use all kinds of stones, pictures, cards, or other physical objects to feel connected to God, but in the end, know you are the power behind these objects. They are only objects to get you back to the One Source. He also said, *many will have different ideas but if they lead to the same ideal, neither one is wrong.*

I think that about sums it up for religion and spirituality. There are at least as many belief systems as there are people here on Earth. There is room for all of them. The dark side helps us see the light side. The good helps us recognize the evil so we can not only heal it but learn from it. This is the way we advance our souls and the human race. We look at what is going on around us and if we don't like it, we change it.

We might change laws. We might change our minds. We might change our beliefs. We might change partners. We might change our sex. We might change everything about us, but you are still you and only you can walk a path that makes you happy and fulfills your life. Only you can take the responsibility for your actions, thoughts and deeds.

So religion and spirituality are very good basis for a foundation of some kind. They help us form what we believe in. They help us to see things clearly no matter which one we believe in. They help us to feel like we belong to something. They give us hope. They give us a reason to continue on. They both do a lot of good and bad; however, they're only systems to help us. They should change with the times and the different things we learn as we grow and discover new things. They shouldn't be set in stone.

Stories from the past are just that, stories from the past. They are learning lessons for us to look at and see what someone else has learned. These stories are a way of helping us learn a lesson through someone else's experiences so we don't have to go through the same pain of learning it.

Religion and spirituality have been around for as long as there have been people. Most of them have grown, changed, evolved but some are still fighting what is happening today and don't want to change. The ones that make us live in fear and in the past are now falling by the wayside. We are entering a new age of believing more in ourselves and the power we have, rather than in the sins of someone eating an apple three thousand years ago.

As I write this book, the growth of religion seems to be at a standstill. People are looking for something other than the stories of the past. They want something that makes sense in this fast paced world. They want something to tell them how to cope with the stresses of today. They don't want to walk through the dark night of the soul just to be saved. They want action and they want it now. This is the way of spirit whether it's religion or spirituality; however, religion tells you to pray and wait. Spirituality tells you to ask and it is done.

Religion differs a lot when it comes to the belief of reincarnation. Some believe in it and some don't. In spirituality, there is a very strong belief in life after death and coming back as many times as you want or need too.

Some religions tell us we won't go to heaven until the second coming of Christ, which in my way of thinking would be reincarnation. Some say we die and sleep until Christ comes again and then we can all ascend into heaven together.

Well, I don't believe in heaven or hell so I guess I don't believe we sleep until there's a second coming of anyone. I know I'll live forever and that my soul travels at night. It doesn't need rest because it's pure energy and therefore when my physical body dies, it just keeps going. Sleep is not something the other side needs nor do they want, as far as I can tell. Sleep is a third dimensional condition.

I believe we can come back as many times as we want because this also involves free will. Living just once and then dying makes no sense to me. If that was what we really did, there would be no point to living. I think the world and universe shows us over and over again that there is life after death. Everything in this world renews its self in some way if we just look at it more closely.

That's my take on religion and spirituality. It really boils down to what do you believe? Are you hurting anyone in your belief system? Are you helping anyone in your belief system? Are you trying to force someone to believe like you do? Are you walking your path or someone else's?

A belief system is as individual as you are and only you have the control over your belief system. Only you have control over who you let into your life and why you're letting them in. Only you can determine if you want to follow their ways or create your own ways of doing things. Only you can determine what is right for you. Make your life simpler by being yourself and not trying to be someone else. Walk the path that is comfortable for you without harming others and you have it.

I feel religion, as we know it today, will go though a big change in the next hundred years. Even in other countries where belief systems are so much stronger than ours here in the US. The world will have to start looking at what is real and what in their system is outdated and not working for them any longer. The age of change has been going on since the beginning of time. We are all changing and growing and expanding and learning. Some day we will understand that we are here to enjoy Earth and all it has to offer us.

I don't feel we'll get there soon because there's still too many beliefs from the past that are still in place and people live in fear of change. If we just understood that change is good, we would be in a better place. Change means the loss of power to many and that creates fear which in turn keeps us stuck in our old belief systems and patterns.

Try to embrace a belief system that doesn't run on fear, insecurity, unhappiness and lies. Step out of fear, be secure in yourself, make your own happiness and belong to yourself. This is the true meaning of religion and spirituality. Worship your life and what you do every day and be thankful you are here experiencing this life. It really doesn't matter who made you, where you came from or even where you're going. It just matters what you do and think today.

Belief systems in the future will have to deal with a number of factors and we're already moving toward these factors today.

1. The role of science is going to be making a big difference in what we believe. As we grow, uncover the past and move toward the future, science is going to be the number one influence in what we can really believe in. Science is going to show us there are energies around that we haven't even begun to understand. I think science will prove ghosts, telepathy, time travel and many other things – maybe even aliens.

2. Technology is another major factor in how we will see things and believe in them. Technology is moving so fast it's almost scary.

3. Population changes will be another factor. As the population grows or decreases, there will be changes because of what the majority or minority believes and how those changes affect the rest of the population in any city, town or country. Population changes also has an affect on the human consciousness of the world. This shift in consciousness will be interesting to watch as the population of the Earth changes.

I feel technology and science are going to be the belief systems of the future. I just hope we don't get so carried away by them we forget one thing – the human condition. We can believe in many things but the main thing we should always believe in is our self. No science or technology, god, goddess, spirit or belief system should ever take the place of our intuition, feelings or creativity. After all, that's why we're here.

We can get all wrapped up in religion, spirituality, science and technology but keep it simple by listening to your inner voice and believing in yourself.

Sin vs. Karma

The concept of sin requires someone on the outside telling you what they determine as "good" or "bad". "Good" or "bad" are concepts and not realities. They are opinions. Sin is something humans made up to be able to label our actions so that the majority of the population can have some sense of what other people consider right or wrong. Sin is telling people what is accepted by most people however, these actions will change with each different belief system, culture and even country. This makes it hard to live without sin.

Sin is a judgment. Sin is used in many cases as a way of controlling our actions, thoughts and words. Sin is used to make us feel bad, unworthy, afraid or just not good enough. Sin is used to make some people right and others wrong. Sin is confusing because it can change with the times or the area you live.

Sin is a sin itself if you really look at it. Nothing in this life should make us feel this bad. Sin is a man-made concept and I feel that "this too shall pass" as we walk forward into the future of our humanness.

Sin is a reward or punishment system. That means that "someone", whether it's God, another person, or a goat, has the ability to judge what you do. If you look at the religions of the world, there could be many different kinds of sins from religion to religion.

An example is the Christian movement in the United States against the Native people. The Christians told the Natives that their religion was wrong. They called them savages and sinners yet the Christians were the first to kill and scalp the Natives. The Natives only started scalping the white man after they saw the white men do it to them.

When the Natives saw the white men scalping their dead, they thought it was some kind of ritual or religious belief. The Native Americans thought if they took the white man's scalp it would somehow be against their Gods and the white man wouldn't be able to enter his afterlife. So even though it was the white man that taught the natives about scalping, the white men called them savages for doing it.

Christians forced the Indians into their religion. They forced them to wear what they thought was a "proper" dress. They forced their ways and their beliefs on them, yet these same Christian people didn't follow their own beliefs. They were rude. They were not a loving, caring group of people. They used force. They killed just because someone was different or didn't do what they told them to do. They were in fear of the Natives, so they had to control them.

Is this the way it is today? Many religious leaders and people will talk the talk but not walk the walk. They think if they go to church or do something in the name of "God" it's okay. This is where "sin" has its downfall. If a certain action or thought is a sin for one person, than it should be a sin for all people – there can't be a select group that doesn't play by the "sin" rules.

Karma on the other hand is not a reward or punishment system. There is no judgment; it's simply the law of cause and effect. It says what you think, do, and say will attract the same energy. This is the law of the Universe and no one can get away from it. Karma says that whatever you do will come back to you with the same amount of energy or intent.

If you are always thinking negative thoughts and think nothing is good, you will get things that aren't good. If you are suspicious and hostile, you will, simply by the nature of this energy, be lonely and unhappy. The people you'll attract will be like you, suspicious and hostile. This is not a fun crowd to be around and this kind of energy creates all kinds of drama and trauma in your life.

Many religions tell us that we can't enter heaven if we have even one sin. Well if we are born into sin, we might as well not even be born. If we are doomed from the start, why live at all? If we have to be free of sin to go to heaven, then there must be a great population in hell. But then again as I have stated earlier, I don't believe in heaven or hell, just a transition from one dimension to another.

I just laugh and shake my head when someone tells me I was born in sin. I figure if I was born in sin, I would have been born with a fig leaf covering me. After all, isn't that what the story of Adam and Eve is about too; covering up our sins.

In spirituality there is a saying, "God doesn't judge us because he knows we judge ourselves way too much as it is."

When we cross, we understand this. Dying is just another way to get back to the source of non-physical energy we call our souls. When we are in the human body we forget we have this energy. This is the energy that runs our body. This is the "source" of our life and the energy that says we are perfect just the way we are, even if we are humans that have to judge everything "good' or "bad'.

Sin is a concept and karma is a reality. Man did not make up karma. The Universe has been working this way for millions and probably billions of years. The rule of "every action has an equal reaction" is simple. It's not a guessing game like sin. It makes life easy if you understand it. Earth is supposed to be a joyful place of experiencing contrasts that we can't experience in the non-physical form.

Think about it. We can't experience eating if we aren't in the physical body. We can't experience walking, running, kissing, touching, writing, disease, sex, animals, and the list goes on and on. We are energy beings having a human experience. Before we incarnate, we look forward to the challenges and the contrasts that Earth provides for us.

We are here to experience and we can all do this in a joyful way – you just have to think you can. It really is as easy as thinking better thoughts.

Our human brain is a terrible thing to waste. We are under the misconception that we only use 10% of our brain; however, this might be wrong. Scientists are studying the brain and their findings are very interesting. These studies are showing we use more of the brain than previously thought. They are finding that certain areas of the brain are used for certain things. Each part of the brain is important but not all of it is used in a conscious way. Much of it is programmed to work on its own without inference from us.

However, these studies are always showing that if we practice enough, we can control some of the ways the brain works. Buddhist monks are showing us that with practice and time, we can control our entire body, mind and soul. We can get in touch with the energies that run our body and have control over them. The problem is not many of us have the time or even take the time to meditate or talk to our body or mind or soul on a regular basis.

If more people really understood how this simple process of quietly getting in touch with ourselves worked and did it everyday, the results would be amazing. It would mean thousand and millions of people would start believing they are smarter than they thought they were. It would mean we can move out of the dogma that has been spread for hundreds of years and get into the truth. This could lead to a whole new way the human race thinks and does things. This could be the beginning of a great new adventure for everyone.

Just by changing this one fact of life, everything can change. This is what spirituality is all about. It's about change and moving forward with what we are learning and living today - not what we did yesterday.

Sin says you have to ask to be forgiven and pay a price. Karma says there is nothing to forgive, just a price to pay. Sin says you can do the same thing over and over and be forgiven if you ask. Karma says you can do the same thing over and over and you will get the same thing back. If you have been nasty or hateful in the past, you will get it back. If you start living a joyful life now, you can lessen a lot of the negative karma you created in the past. You will still have to experience some of what you put out in the past, but it might not be as bad coming back to you as when you put it out there.

In my belief system, there is no sin and no judgment, just karma. This is why I don't judge because I don't want judgment back. I can feel a love for everything even if I don't understand it. I can love someone so much I don't care what they think. I can walk away from situations that are uncomfortable for me and still allow it be what it is. This is living your life and your truth.

Here again, the concept of being born in sin doesn't make sense to me. If we are part of a perfect God, and we are considered his children whom he loves with unconditional love, why would he want us to be born in sin and have to suffer all our lives? No parent wants that for their children.

Sin makes life more complicated. It makes us wonder about our thoughts and question ourselves about our actions. We start to wonder if doing things our way is a sin because it's different from everyone else.

It makes us feel dirty. It gives us a sense of loss and aloneness. Many religions want us to air our sins in public and ask to be forgiven. Again this is control and a way of making us feel we are wrong or bad. This is not what we are here to experience.

Karma says do what you want - just remember you'll get it back. It's very clear and we don't have to question our thoughts or actions. We know right from the start what is going to happen to us. It can happen behind closed doors too. You don't have to tell anyone what you did or didn't do. The Universe knows what energy you put out or didn't put out and the intent behind it. It will bring back whatever you put out even if no one else knows about it. You could receive it in your bedroom and no one would even know.

Religions want you to "share" your sins with the world or at least with a preacher or priest. This is not necessary in spirituality. Spirituality says you know what you did and why and that's all that matters. You'll get it back one way or another and no one has to witness it or know it. It really takes the drama out of life because you are the only one that knows why something is happening to you.

As far back as we have records, we can see karma coming back to individuals, tribes, nations and continents. Sins seem to have some boundaries, limitations, and unreal expectations. Karma is simple. Karma just is. Sin has to be explained and even after explaining it, you have questions. Karma can be explained simply and it works simply. What you put out, you get back. What could be simpler?

I also don't believe in the sins of the past, or of our fathers. The only way the sins of our fathers can affect us, is if we live them too. If we learn from then and choose to not do what they did, we are breaking the pattern and changing the way we live. We are creating our own life, not the life of our parents.

Making people believe we are tied to "our father's sins" is just another way of control and fear. It's a way of saying, "you are now responsible for what everyone did in the past, even if you weren't around at the time." That's horse pucky! We are not responsible for anyone except ourselves. We can learn from someone else's mistakes and that's a good thing.

When we watch other people and how they live their life, it can affect us in a positive or a negative way. It can teach us lessons and how we want or don't want to live our lives. We learn from our parents if we want to be like them or not like them. We learn from our friends in the same way. We learn from strangers to be nice or nasty.

We are always learning, growing and expanding ourselves. We are here to expand our knowing and understanding, and without the experiences and contrast adventures that only Earth can provide for us, we can't do it.

This learning and growing is what life's all about. We've been held back too long by the dogma of how we are supposed to live and the fear of what might happen if we don't do as we are told, instead of living and enjoying.

Some religions say we can't listen to music or dance. This is nuts to me. Tribes as far back as we have recorded history enjoyed this type of relaxation and meditation. Our man-made rules have made this thing we call life too complex. We've lost the original concept of why we came here in the first place.

We didn't come here to be born into sin and spend the rest of our lives trying to get out of it or heal it. We didn't come here to get rich or suffer. We didn't come here to rely on what others tell us to do and how they want us to live our lives. We didn't come here to do anything but experience what we want to experience the only way we can - in human form.

We're supposed to be happy. That was the whole idea around the Garden of Eden story and many other stories of the past. We are supposed to be enjoying this experience. We are supposed to be looking at what we want to create in this physical dimension and then doing it with the best intention and actions we can.

Because we are being told we have sin and we aren't good or there's something wrong with us, we start believing it. This usually happens at a very young age because our parents are trying to scare us into being good. Then it takes 20 to 50 years, maybe never, to get back to knowing this is a lie. It can take a lifetime to get to know our own life source and realize there's nothing wrong with us. The only thing wrong is we have been listening to others and tried to live our lives like they wanted us to. Once we get back to our own source, we can again live how we want to with unconditional love.

This love doesn't mean we have to love everyone or have them in our lives or even understand them. It means you don't judge them for what they do. You know they are living the life they came here to live. It means you don't have worry about anyone else except yourself.

Relationships can be hard when it comes to living our own lives. We want to please our partner but remember, no one can make someone else happy if they don't want to be happy. We shouldn't bend over backwards to try and make someone happy because that will never work for us or for them. If we make ourselves happy and our partner is still unhappy, then it's up to them to either get happy or move on. Remember, nothing lasts forever and every relationship helps us to grow and learn.

The relationship I just got out of was one of a painful lesson for me but I have finally learned it. I can look back on it and be thankful I had it and can see what it did for me. Even though it was difficult at the time and I stayed in a resentful place for awhile, I now see how strong it made me and I can honestly say I'm glad it happened. It was me holding on to a fear and when I let it go, it worked out for the best.

Many religions are finally starting to look at relationships in a different way too. It used to be that living together without being married was a huge sin and having a baby if you weren't married was almost a crime. This kind of thinking is slowing changing and it needs too. There is no sin in living with someone. People come and go in our lives and we have to recognize it's supposed to be that way.

Living together is one way of getting to know each other. You never really know someone until you live with them and sometimes not even then. Humans can hide many things about themselves for a long time. Living with someone is a great way to see if you can spend the rest of your life with them before you get tangled up in all the man-made laws that surround a marriage.

Remember, nothing is set in stone. Everyone changes as they grow and live. There will be differences of opinions or beliefs. There will be times you'll like your partner and times you don't. People are brought into our lives for different reasons and sometimes they are only supposed to be there for a short time. Marriage is a man-made event and even in the beginning it was not because two people loved each other.

Let's take a look at marriage as one example of how things have changed and how wrong it is to judge whether this man-made institution should be the event that makes a difference in our relationships. I believe whether you are the same sex or different sexes, a meeting and sharing of the body, mind and soul is much deeper than a ring around your finger.

There is evidence to suggest that the first marriages took place about 4,300 to 5,000 years ago. Before that, it's believed that families consisted of loosely organized groups. These groups had about 30 people in them with several male leaders. These men shared the women and the women shared the men. Children could have been fathered by any of the men.

There is evidence to suggest that different groups of people had different ways of living. There could have been single unions of one man and woman, two men or two women we really don't have all the information to show us exactly what was going on back then and I don't think it really matters. These groups were wanderers and traveled around from one spot to another depending on the weather, food and water.

As civilizations began to settle down and stay in one place, other "social" arrangements came into play. It was in Mesopotamia that we find the first recorded evidence of marriage ceremonies with a man and woman. From there, marriage spread wide and was embraced by the ancient Hebrews, Greeks and Romans; however, back then it had very little to do with love.

The main purpose was to bind a woman to a man to guarantee that any offspring would be the man's biological heirs. It was through marriage that a woman became the property of a man, not his loving and equal spouse.

A father might hand his daughter over to a man with these words, "I pledge my daughter for the purpose of producing legitimate offspring." But even though many men were married, they were free to take several wives. They were also free to satisfy their sexual urges with prostitutes, concubines and male lovers while the wife stayed home and tended to the house and children. And heaven forbid if the woman didn't produce children! She would be cast aside and the husband could marry someone else. It was automatically her fault, not his.

The above example shows how men ruled and made sin into a gender event. If women had an affair, she sinned but the men saw having relationships with different women their right, not a sin. This kind of thinking is still in the world today and this is the kind of thinking we need to get rid of.

When marriage was brought into the church, it did finally improve the position of the wife. The men were taught to show some respect for their wives. The men were also forbidden from divorcing them. The Christian doctrine, "the twain shall be one flesh" gave both the man and wife exclusive access to each other's body.

Love didn't enter the picture in marriage for years. Much of human history says people came together for practical reasons, not because they loved each other. When love entered the picture, it helped change the role of women again. Wives were no longer just a servant or child provider to their husbands. It actually took until the 1920's here in the United States to really bring marriage into what it is today. When woman won the right to vote, she was then looked on as almost an equal to her husband.

Now I think many women look at marriage as a way to get a man and keep him, just the same way it was looked on by men thousands of years ago. It seems we might have come full circle here. We should understand that no one is really ever ours or belongs to us. We belong to "ourself" and that is the only thing we really ever have in our life.

There was a time in the second and third centuries in Roman history when homosexual weddings were so common the social commentator of the time, Juvenal, was worried it would never end. He wrote, "Such things, before we're very much older, will be done in public." The Romans formally outlawed homosexual marriages in the year 342 but many gay marriages continued through the Catholic and Greek Orthodox churches.

So as you see, same sex marriages are not a new thing. We don't know why some of us are gay and some of us aren't but it doesn't really matter. We might be reliving a past feeling or we might have wanted to be that way from the start to experience what it feels like to be gay, bi-sexual or maybe not even want sex. Who knows? And no one should really care! If it's not your life, let it be.

I don't feel it's a sin to judge others, because, like I've said, I don't believe in sin, but karma will get you for judging them. Taking this one example, we can see how humans can take a union of two people and turn it around, upside down, inside out and backwards until it's no longer what it's supposed to be; a union between two people who love each other.

There was no marriage until man settled into communities and started forming cities. I look at marriage as another way people control each other, if they want to. There are marriages out there where the people don't look at the marriage as ownership, but only a very few. In my book, if you are living with someone, you are in a committed relationship and that should be enough to keep you from being with someone else.

We could go on and on about different things that are considered sins, but the only thing we should remember is that sins can be made to be anything anyone wants. Sins can be made up and changed as we change. Sins are not set in stone. Maybe the Ten Commandments were said to be "set in stone" by God as a metaphor. Someone wanted us to think these rules were set in stone so they couldn't be changed, but that will never happen in this world. Everything is in a constant change.

It seems different situations call for different sins to make us feel guilty. The thing I don't understand is that different sins have different punishments. Now who thought of this? What makes one sin worse than another? Is murder any worse than rejecting your spouse for someone else? Each will result in a death. One is the death of a person and one is death of a relationship.

Karma says all bad or good deeds will come back to you with the same amount of force you put into them. Karma doesn't judge if the deeds are bad or good or big or small. It depends on the energy you put behind the deed, the thought or something you said that will determine how it comes back to you. This way no one person or organization can judge what your punishment or reward should be. There is no bias or favoritism. There is just the same energy coming back to you that you put out. It makes life so much simpler.

So there you have it – my take on sin vs. karma. Sin is man-made and can vary to the point you don't know if you are sinning or not. It keeps you off balance; this is the way many religions like it because it takes your power away and they have control over you. Sin is a judgment and concept that you can never live up to or get away from. Everything you do can be looked at as a sin if someone says it is. It's not consistent nor does it make sense to me.

Karma is a rule of the universe. It's consistent, it's complete, there's no judgment – it just is. It's easy to understand because you are the only one that is responsible for what you do, think or say. Karma will be fulfilled no matter what. The only thing that determines how it comes back to you is you! No one else can tell you how bad or good it was because karma is built on your own intention of the action you are doing or the thought you are having. What could be simpler?

Karma makes it so we don't have to wonder what our punishment will be or if someone else will find out what we did. No one has to tell us what we need to do to be "forgiven". Karma is just karma. We can have good karma for thinking good, kind thoughts and doing deeds that are good; or we can have bad karma for thinking bad, nasty thoughts, saying nasty things to or about people or doing nasty deeds. It's really that simple.

Sin holds us in fear. Karma tells us like it is. Sin gives us a choice and so does karma. Sin tells us to live by someone else's rules and laws. Karma tells us to live by the laws of the universe. Sin tells us we could go to hell if we are not forgiven. Karma tells us there is no hell except for what we make here on Earth. Sin is a fear, karma is a fact.

Religions say you can ask for forgiveness of your sins and get it. Karma says change your thoughts and actions and change your karma. I believe there is no need to ask for forgiveness from a higher power. You can say you're sorry for thinking bad thoughts or for doing bad deeds but until you really mean it and start changing your ways, karma will still bring you what you put out.

There are some religions that tell us if we repent our sins, we are forgiven. Who forgives us? God? The person we did something too? Did we go to them and ask for forgiveness? What if they don't forgive us? Would that mean we have to carry that sin around for the rest of our lives? And what if we keep doing the same thing over and over again? How many times can we ask for forgiveness for the same thing?

If a person is a liar and they go to church and repent that sin, what good is it if they do it again? Karma says, lie all you want because you will get lies in return. Once you stop lying, you will start getting the truth. Religions can forgive us a hundred times for something but it doesn't mean anything until we stop doing it.

My higher power says, "Do your best with what you know at the time and don't intentionally hurt anyone or anything. Don't do something good just to get back goodness. Do something good because it makes you feel good. Do something because you want to help someone, something or some place."

If we started doing good deeds just because it felt good without worry about sin or even karma, we would live a more joyful, happy life. Karma or sin – you be the judge of which one you want to have in your life. After all you're the only one who can choose.

What if Science was our Religion?

When I first asked myself "What if science was our next religion?" I saw the Wizard of Oz that Dorothy, the tin man, the scarecrow and the lion talked to. I could see that big head on the wall, in my mind's eye, and thought about our big screen TVs and had to laugh. I laughed because I think this is what many of us are coming too. Not only do we watch too much TV but we believe too much of what we see on it.

My next thought was about how science is like the big head; it's only a tool to the truth of the moment. Science lives in the now and changes with new discoveries. Believing only in science is like putting all your faith into only one religion or belief system. There are just too many variables to say any one belief system is right or wrong.

There are so many directions science can take us and we can get confused with all the facts or theories. It's just like religion. There are over 6200 recognized religions today. Who's to say which one is right and which one is wrong?

Science is only another way to look at stories from the past and figure out many things about Mother Earth, ourselves, the present and the future. Science has at least the same number of options as religions to figure things out and it has one option most religions don't have. Science has the option to change its mind as it learns more about something.

We should remember that religion isn't perfect and neither is science. Scientists show us theories one day and then have it questioned or disproven when more information is available. This should be a great reminder not to jump to conclusions about anything in this world or this dimension.

Take my line of work for example. Many people don't believe in animal communication or psychic readings because they can't be proven. I say that's okay because one day science will prove it and then our beliefs will change too.

Nothing ever stays the same and science is the medium that is proving that fact. Life is discovering and learning and then changing with each new discovery. Change is about movement and energy. When you change your thoughts, you change your energy and you discover many different things.

There are energies all over this universe we don't understand. They're invisible. We don't see them, nor do we have the technology or equipment right now to prove they even exist. I also believe that we will never "prove" them all because they are forever changing.

Just like in the Wizard of Oz, Dorothy, the tin man, the scarecrow and the lion had to prove only to themselves they had the qualities they were looking for. They had been searching on the outside for something they already had on the inside. This was what their journey to the Emerald City was all about.

This is what our life is all about. It's a journey of discovering and experiencing things and then deciding if it's what we want or what we don't want in our lives. This journey is how we prove to ourselves what we can and can't do. Just like the actors in the Wizard of Oz who learned about their own power, we have to do the same. They learned the truth about themselves. They learned they could achieve many things when they put their minds to it. They learned miracles began with them and their actions. It just took a wise person, who was the man behind the big head, to point this out to them.

Many times we call events miracles but they are really just what is supposed to happen at that time. There is nothing mysterious about them. We are so used to not seeing the real meaning of life; we forget that miracles, in many cases, are just events we are seeing for the first time.

When it comes to faith or science, many times we put our faith in science instead of our selves. Just like science, when we find out the truth or reason behind any situation or mystery, the illusion of it being strange or weird disappears. This "learning" will also make any fear about the event disappear too.

Science is showing us that many things are supposed to happen and have been happening that way for thousands of years. To see it on paper makes sense to our human brain. Because our brain is human and part of the physical world, many things called "miracles" don't make sense to the brain. Events or happenings that are related to the spiritual world may seem confusing or "something that can never happen."

This can confuse us and we start to look for answers that may not be able to be answered. Some religious and even spiritual leaders use this "humanness" as a way of controlling people through the fear of not understanding what is really happening.

More people are beginning to understand that energy runs everything on this Earth and in this universe so they are starting to understand why many things happen. This is one good thing science is doing for us, but we have to remember that science still can't provide us with all the answers. Science is a man-made adventure and so it too is not perfect. Only your soul is perfect and that's why it's more important to know yourself and why you're here, rather than to understand every event that takes place in your life and around the world.

We can spend millions of years exploring the Universe and other worlds that are in space but the real adventure is getting to know who we are and why we're here. Science shows us there are more dimensions than just the 2nd, 3rd, and 4th. When science has a better understanding of these dimensions and how they work, we'll all start to understand how energy and dimensions affect our lives.

Right now we're in the 3rd dimension with a third dimensional body so the only way to visit the other dimensions is to get out of our body. (There are energy vortexes where you can go in and out very quickly with your body but that's a whole other book and something science is still working on.) It's hard for the human body to stay in another dimension because it's meant for this dimension.

When we're in spirit, we don't have a human body, a human brain or anything that's human. When we're in spirit, we're in our energy body, also known as the soul. Because this energy body has a higher vibration than our human body, we live in a different dimension.

Pascal, a 17th century philosopher, said humans were made of 3 parts; mind, body and soul. Science only deals with the first two at this point of our human development. Science can explore most of the physical world but has problems when it comes to the unseen world of spirit.

It's hard to "prove" anything about the spirit world at this point. Our energy body, or soul, was made for the other dimensions but because we live in the human body, our human brain has trouble understanding the energy world.

I believe that each dimension is different and we have to adjust our vibration to match it. This is all part of our life as souls.

So why are we here? We are here to experience events, food, emotions, touching and all the other things we can't experience in the same way when we are in a different dimension. Each dimension has its own experiences and ways to experience events.

Almost everything we experience in this dimension is different from any other dimension. Our humanness can't understand that. Our human brain can't understand things in a different dimension because it can't go there. Our brain is supposed to function in the third dimension and understand things that happen there. I don't think we have evolved to the point where the human brain can understand a lot of the other dimensions – but we're getting there.

When we close our minds to possibilities, we are closing our minds to everything that can happen in other dimensions. Even when you close your mind to other religions or spiritual beliefs, it cuts you off from many truths and events or miracles. There are some things that work the way they are supposed to work because that's just how they work. It's not weird or wrong or right or anything. It just is the way it is. Only humans want to dissect everything to see what makes things tick.

Science and technology are great, but it can take over. It's like anything else in this world; moderation is a good thing. Being radical about anything is not a good or even a healthy balance. There are many things we can't prove at this time, so relax.

Let's use love as an example of how we try to prove something. Love is an emotion, a feeling; something you can't see. You can only prove love by the amount of effort you expand on behalf of the person you love. The same is true for hate, grief and all other emotions. However this measurement is only a 3rd dimensional action of a 4th or 5th dimensional feeling. There really is no scientific way to measure love.

So asking someone to show their love or trying to measure it scientifically can't be done. Their actions might suggest love but actions are only actions. Actions are how we express ourselves in this dimension.

Actions are a physical manifestation of our emotions. Because humans are so visual, we need to see things to feel they're real.

Science works by challenging what is suggested. If an idea or theory can be reproduced by others, it's accepted as a law or truth. The problem with that is when new facts are brought forth, the law or truth can and has changed. Science, like true spirituality, is an ever changing and growing world of discovery.

Science can be helpful in our learning but there are many things that will change as we discover new things about the Earth and the ever changing universe we live in. Nothing stays the same in this universe except our souls. This is one reason why science can relate more to our souls than religion. Many religions refuse to look at the changing times, the changing energies, the changing thoughts and the new facts that keep getting discovered.

Right now science and technology are so much a part of our daily lives, and we feel we can't live without them. Let's take a look at what people are doing right now as they walk down the street. Most of them are either talking on a cell phone or texting someone. What have we become? We don't know how to be alone anymore. I think we're afraid to be alone. Alone somehow means we are not successful or loved.

We don't know what it's like to just let the phone ring or not answer a text message. I've heard people say that a person is bullying them on their text messaging. Have we forgotten there is a delete button?

We get so caught up in the lies or lives of others that we can't even see our own. It seems we never have a moment to ourselves because we create so much drama and commotion in our lives. We don't take the time to think things through. In this fast paced world many times we react to something before we think through what our actions will bring back to us.

If we aren't working, we're talking; texting or worrying about what comes next. Humans are the only animals that can talk all day long about nothing. Our talk is cheap and most of the time it means nothing. People have lost the ideal of what a promise or keeping their word means. We've gotten so used to talking, we aren't listening anymore, unless it's to the TV, and everything on TV seems to be negative.

Let's look at phones as just one example. We're programmed from a very young age to answer the phone when it rings. We don't have to answer it, but we have been programmed to answer it. However, science has come up with several ways to help us with this compulsion. Voice messaging and phone answering machines were invented for a reason and it's okay to use them. This is one way science is giving us more choices. We need to start using these choices. Even text messages can be saved and answered or deleted later.

Are we worshiping technology with each of these products because we think we can't live without them? Does that make science and technology a religion right now?

Could it be that science is really telling us we are connected through our energies and souls and these devices are just an extension of that connection? It's something to think about.

We know through these devices we can keep in touch with our loved ones no matter where we are. In spirituality we understand we are all connected by Source and can communicate any time we want too. We've gotten so used to using these other devices, we have unplugged our natural ability to communicate through telepathy. The good news is we can all plug that cord back in and start using it any time we want too.

We, as humans, don't feel connected unless we are touching, talking or texting someone. Humans have to see something to believe it and this is where science comes in. Science is our playground of exploring and experiencing. It's a way many things can be explained and either recreated or written down for us to see so we can believe it.

I find it amazing as an animal communicator that the animals can smell something, hear something or just be aware of something and they know it exists. They don't question it like humans do. If a rabbit smells a fox, he goes in the opposite direction because he knows it's really there. If humans smell a bear in the woods, they go toward it because they have to prove to themselves it's really there. That's insanity. We don't trust our natural instincts any more.

Maybe we don't trust ourselves because science and technology have us questioning everything – there is a negative side to everything positive so science has its good and bad points too. Take the smell of bacon. When you smell it you might have to ask yourself if it's real pork bacon, beef bacon, turkey bacon, or tofu bacon. We don't know until we see it or taste it.

Science and technology are great but have we gone too far with them? Have we invented too many things that look like the real thing but aren't? Are we are losing our natural instincts and the ability to believe in what we can't see or prove? Are we being told anything that isn't proven can't be real? Are we losing our imagination? Are we losing our trust in us?

We should remember not to put all our trust in any one thing; whether it's religion, spirituality or science. There are truths in all of them but believing in just one thing or one way of doing something limits your ability to see other ways of doing things. It limits your thoughts and your creative side. If there is one thing we should be aware of it's that there are as many ways to do something or to believe in as there are people and animals on this planet.

That doesn't make one way right and one way wrong, it just makes them different. It makes them individual and unique. It's what makes each of us who we are. We would be a very boring species of we all did the same thing the same way. Besides, we wouldn't learn anything.

When it comes to doing something our way, we should listen to our inner self more. We all know what we are supposed to do; we just don't listen to ourselves. We listen to the people on the outside instead of listening to the person we have on the inside.

We need to trust the little voice inside our head more. That little voice is there to help us and keep us alive and safe. No science project can prove that, however there are millions of humans walking around today that believe it, know it, and feel it is the truth.

Humans are animals and we need to go back and learn more about our instincts and what they can do for us. Science and technology are great, but they will never be better than our natural instincts. No computer will ever really have the true human emotions or know what the soul knows. They can tell us a lot of things, but when it comes to just "feeling right or wrong"; a computer doesn't have a chance.

We should try to remember we are all connected in some way all the time. You see it on the news every night. People's actions in another country affect us in some way. It affects how we feel or how the world's economy might be affected – which can affect all of us because this world puts so much power into money.

We don't realize that any and all of our actions have some affect on someone or something or someplace on this planet. As I stated earlier, all our actions are physical manifestations of our thoughts or feelings. Each thought, feeling and action starts a chain of events or reactions no matter how big or small.

It's like throwing a rock into a pond. At the entry point, there are big, close ripples of water. As they move through the water, the energy is dispersed in a chain reaction. When the first ripples hit the shore, they are intense with energy but the ripples that follow get less intense. The first ripple will hit the shore hard and can really impact it. And even though the other ripples are not as intense, they too will have an impact on the shore. If the ripples keep gently washing up on the bank, the bank will change.

That's what happens with our energy. When we say, think or do something, the people, animals or objects that are right next to us feel more of the effect. As these words, thoughts or actions move out into the world in the form of energy waves, they lessen. Someone on the other side of the Earth probably won't feel them unless they are very connected to you in the first place.

Every time we breathe we are making a difference in something. Every motion moves some kind of energy and then sets off a chain reaction. Because everything is energy and everything is touching or connected in some way, there has to be a chain reaction.

Just watch some of the reality shows on TV right now and you can see how the actions of one person can affect the rest of the people they are living with. Look at how our own family's actions affect us. Look at how someone at work affects us. If we can't see we are connected through these examples, we need to look again.

Spirituality, science and religion tell us we all connected. Religion tells us we are connected to God and we are all brothers and sisters. Is that why we have so many wars? Are we like siblings that can't seem to get along? Or are wars just what they appear to be – a senseless waste of time, energy and human life just to feed someone's ego. If we're all connected in this thing we call "life", then why kill each other! Aren't we really killing ourselves?

Religion tells us about this connection and then draws lines between one religion and another. It creates friction because it says if you believe in a different religion or God, you're wrong. Even if every religion teaches us we are part of God, each one is basically saying if you don't believe in my God, you're wrong or your God is wrong. How can we be all connected and be from a different source? That's like saying you have an identical twin but different parents.

Right now, science is uncovering more and more about our DNA and other energies we share. Science is showing us in many ways how connected we are. Energy and our DNA are amazing things and we've just scratched the surface of really understanding it. As the human condition evolves and learns, there will come a time when we will understand all of this. That will be the time when we will be ready to move on. We only have about 5 billion years to do this, so we better get going!

Spirituality says we are all from the same Source. It's doesn't matter if you think that Source is God, Goddess, Ali, Buddha or whoever it might be. It says that all these Sources are the same Source. It's all one power, one energy, one thought system, and one connection. It's all the same and we are all the same. This is what science and spirituality are all about; proving or understanding we are all connected in some way. We have just barely touched the surface on understanding the human condition.

However, many religions, in my opinion, tell us we are wrong and separated from each other if we don't believe in the same thing. In my opinion, many religious beliefs hold us back from learning and growing. They want us to live in the past. They want us to think like people did a thousand years ago. We need to move forward from that way of thinking. We are not a race of robots but a race of free thinking and free willed individuals even if we all share the same human DNA.

It's a fact we all share the DNA that makes us human beings – if we didn't we wouldn't be human. We'd be dogs, cats, aliens or something else. DNA plays a big part in who we are and what we are. Every tulip bulb has some of the same DNA that tells them they are tulips. The tulip DNA is different from rose DNA but both have "plant" DNA. The tulip DNA tells it what it should look like when it grows. The DNA says to it, "you are a tulip, not a rose." Then the DNA goes one step farther and tells each tulip what color it's going to be and other individual character traits. That's just like us humans.

We're all humans but our DNA tells us to be a girl or boy or white or black or brown. It tells us what color eyes we are going have, the color of our hair, when we'll go bald and when we'll do just about everything else in our lives. Our individual DNA is all about us but the DNA we share with the rest of the human race tells us no matter what color we are, we are still human. It's time us humans start realizing this.

Dogs don't think other dogs are cats just because they look different or are a different color. Dogs don't judge another dog for its size, color or sex. As humans, we accept dogs as dogs and cats as cats and birds as birds and so on. We group them all together but many times we don't do this with humans. We think if a human looks different from us, they aren't like us. That's not true.

Every human I've talked to wants to live in peace, wants to find a mate who will love them, wants to make a good living and wants to be happy. That alone should show us we are all connected.

As science discovers and uncovers new and different things, we see more of how everyone on this planet has an effect on everyone else. Maybe in a few hundred years we'll know and understand more. Will that be the time when we reject religion and believe in science even more? I think that would be going from one extreme to another but that's what us humans do.

Science is uncovering more history of the Earth everyday. Many of these discoveries are showing the stories of the past are either not true or could not have happened as the story says it did. This will bring up more questions and more opportunities to see the past as something different from what we have been taught throughout time. It starts to give us more truth.

This helps to really understand the powers or the "so-called" miracles that happened in the past. Most of them are actually events that happen once a month or once a year or once every 25,000 years anyway. Science is helping us to understand how the universe works and we don't have to fear most of the falling stars anymore.

Science helps us to understand that many religious beliefs were based on fear of the unknown. As we uncover the mysteries of the past and of the universe, we discover the natural way things work. That takes the mystery out of things so it takes the fear out too. When we don't fear something, we can walk into it with the knowledge of it being okay. Fear is the biggest factor in the human condition that holds us back and keeps us from growing and enjoying the life we came here to experience.

Exploring events, mysteries, the past and the present are all ways science can help us walk through the fear and head in the right direction. We shouldn't fear change because it's one of the only things constant in the universe. Change has been going on since before the beginning of time as we know it and it will continue long after we are gone. That's why we should continue to explore and find out about things.

We haven't explored even half of the oceans and what they hold at the bottom. Land masses still have cities, countries and other places waiting to be unburied and explored. Space, which is really the last frontier, will never be explored to its fullest because there is no end to it.

So if science was our religion, what would it do for us? What would it teach us? What could we believe in? Would it confuse us more because one theory might be true today but not tomorrow? How could we believe in something that changes so often?

I think, like everything else, science has its place in this world. Without it, we would be in the same place we were a hundred years ago. It's good to believe in what science has shown us so far but we have to do it with an open mind. Anything can change at any time.

So what more would we believe in? We already know the world's round. We know about Earthquakes, the seasons, the weather, the tides and climates around the world, but there is so much more to learn about.

We still don't know everything about how the human body works. Each person is different and their body works different from our body in many ways. We don't know how the universe or even our planet works for sure. We have so much more to learn and study.

We need to continue to uncover the past so we can make sense of the present and the future. We need to learn that anything is possible and everything is probable.

Hopefully part of science will help us see that nothing can hold us back if we do it right. If we study the rules of the Universe and understand them, we can do anything.

We would believe in the unseen forces of energy because they would be proven in some way to exist in some form.

We would believe more in ourselves. Science would show us if we focus on energy and use it right, we can manifest anything we want in our lives. Science would show us by focusing on something, whether it's positive or negative, we are asking for that same kind of energy to come back to us.

If we believed only in science, we would be changing our beliefs more often and keeping up with what science was telling us was real at that time. Wow – that could create a lot of panic, anger and many other human emotions that could cause us to become a race of neurotic robots.

However, science could help us with guilt or shame because we could all say, "Wow I didn't know that but now that I do, I can change my mind."

Most religions tell us we have to believe in all the stories of the past whether they are proven right or wrong. That doesn't make sense to me and that way of thinking just holds us in the past with the lies of the past. It holds us in fear of tomorrow and what the future might bring. It's okay to find out what you once thought was true isn't and just move on with the truth at that point.

If we believed just in science, we wouldn't have to hang on to a past that wasn't true or a past that didn't make sense or serve us. We could let go of a lot of baggage we now carry. We could also blame science for not moving fast enough to discover the truth in the first place. (We always have to blame someone for something, don't we? We can't seem to say, "Wow, I'm glad I know that now." And just leave it at that.)

If you really think about it, science is already like a religion now.

In religion you have a priest or clergyman – in science you have doctors or people with the titles of "Dr." In religion you have temples or churches – in science you have hospitals and labs. In many churches, only members of the church can come in. There are limited thoughts and actions in most churches. The same goes with hospitals and labs. They are for medical people and patients that believe in them. The problem with many religions and hospitals is they're stuck in their own ways. Religions are stuck in the teachings of the past and the hospitals are stuck in only Western medicine. Western medicine usually treats a disease, but ignores the cause of the disease.

Many doctors are still treating diseases with only medications and not looking at what might be the underlying cause of the disease in the first place. The "alternative medicine" people don't always agree with all the medications doctors give people because many of these medications just hide the cause of the disease and never really cure it. Most Western medicine, in my opinion, keeps people sick and doesn't allow them to heal or cure whatever is really ailing them. And just look at some of the medicines out on the market today. Their warnings of what could go wrong when you take them are worse than what is ailing you.

Religion, spirituality and science all have their own skeptics and non-believers. That's a good thing. It helps us to keep exploring and learning and growing.

As we move forward into new discoveries, many of our beliefs may be challenged or even proven wrong. It may mean we have to adjust or change what we believe in. This is a hard thing for people to do. When we start to understand that we are all the same, and everyone is here to experience something different, we'll have to change our belief systems and way of thinking.

We might have to look at each individual as a private scientific experiment in progress. Each life needs time to develop, grow and experience what it's supposed to in this lifetime. Each person develops their own theories about life and all the events in this dimension. This takes time and learning and looking into everything we find interesting. Just like most scientific experiments that have any merit, it takes time and patience to find a pattern or truth. Isn't this what life is all about?

The truth of the Universe is always the same. It will never change no matter how old it is. The truth is, everyone's "truth" is different. Your truth is your truth and my truth is my truth. In the end, you will believe what you want to believe and I'll believe what I want to believe and neither of them is right or wrong. They are just beliefs that help us to be who we are and learn what we are supposed to learn in this lifetime.

There is room enough on planet Earth for everyone's truth. There is never just one way to get some place on this planet. There are paths all over and if you can't get there from the ground, then you can fly or take a boat or do something else. That's what spirituality is all about. Finding a way to your truth and living it your way.

Science also has several different ways of looking at and doing things. Just like spirituality, science doesn't rely on "just one writing" or someone's word to try and prove anything. Science and spirituality seem to write life and history as they go and not rely on too much of the past because things change. Science and spirituality work with the unseen as a normal, everyday event, not as an unexplained miracle.

Religion looks at the past to explain the future but many times this doesn't make sense. Many of the Bible stories are like a good fairy tale; they tell a story, have a lesson and moral in it and then it's up to us to decide what it means to us. We can neither live in the past nor the future so the best thing to do is look at what is happening now and see how we can apply it to our lives.

Science is just really beginning to work with energy and things that go bump in the night. Science is starting to understand that just because we can't see it doesn't mean it doesn't exist. Science is just scratching the surface of what really lies between us and the rest of the universe.

In another two or three thousand years we may have a different view of religion, spirituality and science. Hopefully we will have dropped all the horror stories of the past and look at what really happened. Hopefully we'll face the fact that religion is only a man-made tool to keep people in fear. Hopefully we'll all discover we're already part of something greater than ourselves. Hopefully we'll take control of this power again and use it for good - knowing it can work for all of us not just a select few.

Science will one day show us that everything is possible if we just put our wonderful minds to it. It will show us there is something beyond this Universe and this life as a human. I see more people studying, learning and growing as more and more truths are uncovered. This is what people need.

Religion wants us to live in a past we don't remember so many people are losing interest in it. Many times it seems religion is eating us instead of feeding us by telling us "who we are supposed to be and what we are supposed to do" because of some dumb man-made thing called sin. Anything we view as a belief should feed us and allow us to be ourselves and find our own individual path.

Many of the religious stories of the past are not right. Science is beginning to show us this fact. "Miracles" of the past are being shown to be events that were supposed to happen and that continue to happen to this day. History does repeat itself until we learn from the past and start doing things differently. It takes a long time for humans to do this.

People today are looking for miracles just like they were thousands of years ago. It seems when we get into the human condition, we need to have miracles to remind us we are connected to a higher power or something that is greater than our human body.

Religion teaches us that we have to see miracles to have them proven to us. Spirituality says it can be a miracle whether you see it, feel it or just know it. They don't have to be visual. Science says there are no miracles; there is a reason for everything happening and we just haven't found that reason yet.

Science and spirituality should be fun and even religion should be fun. Both science and spirituality are ever changing, ever growing and ever pushing us to improve ourselves. Religion wants us to live in fear. Religion asks us to believe in almost everything except ourselves and how powerful we are. It just makes sense to me if we are the children of a God, we would have some of those God-like qualities.

Science discovers and uncovers the past and dispels our fears. All the new discoveries of science are in the present moment. Spirituality says – live in the present because the past is gone and the future hasn't come yet.

I see science and spirituality as our next religions that can live together, side by side. There is no threat from either of them. They are both looking for the truth. They are both open to new ways. They both take responsibility for what they uncover and move forward with it.

Science and spirit are always on the move forward and looking for new discoveries. They are also moving at a fast pace. Neither stands still like many of the world religions. Most religions are stuck in the ways of the past and many of those ways don't work in this present world and changing times. Even meditation in spirituality has been updated to mean a walk, painting, reading or just being in the present moment so you can view your life from that moment.

Don't get me wrong, I think we all need to pray or meditate or reflect on our lives but we don't need to spend hours doing it. The energy we put out in a single second can do a million miracles. Humans seem to like the drama of taking something very simple and making it very hard.

Humans love drama. I think that's because we don't have drama on the other side. When we die, we just have love and learn more wonderful things; sounds almost boring, doesn't it? However, I've never spoken to a dead person who thinks life on the other side is boring. They have things to do and learn and people to visit.

If we can really remember that we're energy beings living in a human body, we can start to manifest what we want out of life. We can start to see that just by thinking about something or someone it can change our lives.

Just a few minutes ago I had been thinking about a friend and she called. Either she got my message through my thoughts or I got the thought she was putting out about calling me. That's just how simple it's supposed to work.

I'm not asking you to pick between religion, spirituality or science. I'm asking you to find the truth about who you are and what you want out of this life, and then live it in great peace, joy and love.

Whatever your belief – make it simple

Humans are the funniest animals on the planet. We say we want something and then we do everything in our power not to get it.

We all say we want simpler lives but then we do things that complicate it. Take computers for example. They were supposed to put an end to paper but because we are so visual, we still print things out to make sure they're real. I think there will always be some kind of written word because deep down we all know computers crash and data can be lost. The written word has been around for hundreds of thousands of years and it's hard habit to break.

Before written word or in places where there were no caves or walls to write on, we have the spoken words of elders who passed down legends and stories. These stories have been changed and mis-told for years but I believe most of them have some true points about them. But even some of these stories can add confusion and stress to our belief systems of today – mainly because we can't prove if they're true or just stories.

Many of these stories are like baking a cake. They start with some basic ingredients and then things are added and deleted each time they are told. When this happens, you can end up with something that's supposed to be one thing but looks like another.

Let's look at our lives as a recipe in baking a cake. There was a time when our grandmothers and great grandmothers would walk into the kitchen, grab a bowl, a few ingredients and make something great.

She would take some flour, sugar, eggs, vanilla, and baking soda and add a lot of love and make the most wonderful cake you ever tasted. That's just like our life. All we need to do is add our knowledge, wisdom, experiences, the wonder of life and lots of love to see what life is all about.

However, now-a-days, not many of us bake a cake from scratch. We buy one. In fact, many people don't know how to even start to make a cake unless they grab a mix off the grocery shelf. Then they don't look at the ingredients because they just trust whatever's in the mix will end up as a cake if they follow the directions on the box.

So what is in one of these cakes anyway? Here's an example of what might be in it.

Sugar, Enriched Wheat flour bleached, nonfat milk, whole eggs, egg whites, partially hydrogenated vegetable oil, invert sugar, propylene glycol mono and diesters, food starch - modified, leavening (basically baking powder), dextrose, mono and diglycerides, salt, soy lecithin, water, polysorbate 60, sodium propionate (as preservative), xanthium gum, sodium stearoyl lactylate, guar gum, cellulose gum, artificial flavor, corn starch propylene glycol, sugar, vegetable oil, mono and diglycerides, corn starch, natural and artificial flavor, salt guar gum, artificial color, water, cream, salt, sugar, vegetable shortening, water, butter, wheat starch, mono diglycerides, salt, artificial flavor, polysorbate 60.

If you can tell me in 30 seconds or less, without looking it up, what half these ingredients are, you win the smart ass prize of the month. And just look at the sugar! 3 times it's listed. Inverted sugar is just a mix of glucose and fructose syrup. Why do they need all this stuff? Well, most of them are preservatives! Yeah, that's what I want in my body. Pretty soon our bodies will have so many preservatives they'll never break down to dust and future generations will have to deal with a bunch of dead bodies that won't go away.

This is what we have done with religion and our belief systems. We make them so full of drama and things we don't need, we forget the true meaning of it.

We need to make our life and beliefs simple again. When we add drama, hate, anger, worry and co-dependency, we are adding artificial ingredients. We are adding things to the mix that don't need to be there. They can taint the flavor of our lives and make everything seem harder than it is.

The more we add to it, the longer it will take to become something we really want it to be. If you were to just look at the above ingredients without knowing it was a cake, you might be able to figure it out but it could be a recipe for muffins too.

Just like baking, we should know what ingredients are going into our cake and if they are good for us or not. Too many ingredients can spoil a good thing.

The same should be with our belief system. I think we should all know about other religions and beliefs but many of them get so caught up in their own "stuff", they have forgotten what they are supposed to be about.

Almost all religions believe in a higher power or God. They all think "their" god is the only god. Hell, even back in Greek mythology there were several gods and goddesses. Many of the tribes around the world had a god for everything. So why do we believe in only one god now? And whatever happened to the goddesses of old?

In my belief system, I don't have to go to church to pray to God. To me, church is a building we go to too show others we believe in something. It's not God's house. God doesn't need a house – humans need houses. God's house is this Universe and for all we know all of outer space might be his home. What would he want with a building? It's just a building and a gathering of people. We can do that with anything. I don't need to show other people I believe in a higher power. I don't need to show anyone anything.

I can go to God's house in the hills and pray or in the shower or my backyard or just anywhere I want to. I don't want someone else knowing that I'm praying or why or what I'm praying for. That's a very personal thing between me and my God, angels, masters, teachers, helpers and spirit guides. I have enough people on the other side that can hear and see me, I don't need anyone on this side seeing me.

Making your belief system simple can really simplify your life. I believe that once I ask for something, it will be given. I believe that when I talk to the heavens, everyone that supposed to hear me does. I believe miracles happen everyday without any reason for them. I believe I don't have to believe like anyone else to be right. I believe in letting everyone believe however they want as long as they aren't hurting someone else.

I don't do a lot of ceremony in my meditations or prayers, but many people do. Whatever people need to do to get closer to their higher self and their God is just fine with me. Many need these ceremonies and many of these ceremonies have been passed down from generation to generation and should be honored and remembered but they aren't for everyone.

If someone asks me what I believe, I tell them but I don't go into great detail or try to "recruit' them into my beliefs. I don't expect them to believe what I do. I don't tell them what to believe and I don't care what they believe. It's a personal choice and a personal belief.

Making your life simpler is easy if you just step back from it and look at what you are doing everyday. I used to try and get as much done in one day as I could and I soon found I was tired all the time.

Now I get done what I can because I know there will always be something else to do no matter how much I do.

My life is simpler and everyday I try to do something else that makes it even easier than the day before. Life is supposed to be simple. We are here to live, learn, experience, expand our knowledge and have fun while we are doing it. If we worry too much about how everything works, we can't have fun.

However, there always has to be a balance. Too much fun can mean you aren't playing attention to some chores that might need done. It doesn't mean you have to do chores all the time but if you party all the time, something will come of it and it might not be very positive. I tell people have fun while you are doing your chores or working and then they become fun instead of a chore.

You can change everything you do with just a change of your thoughts. Instead of looking at it as a chore, look at it as something that will benefit you when its done. Everything we do benefits us in some way. It's pretty simple – everything on Earth is supposed to be simple. Even the way the Universe works is simple and it does it over and over again. We just judge it as complicated or over-whelming and when we do this, it creates drama in our lives. Drama is usually something we don't understand so it creates stress and that leads to drama, trauma and many other emotions.

If you get simple about thinking about things, this will change the energy around you and you'll find things will begin to get easier.

It helps me to talk to my guides and angels and ask them to help me or talk to me. Sometimes if you focus on the chore you are doing, it helps too. You'll find an easier way or different way of doing it and the boredom of it goes away because you are learning something.

There are all kinds of ways to make your life simpler. Owning a lot of "toys" might make your life easier but then again, they may not. You usually have payments or insurance costs. You have to worry about them breaking or falling apart or someone stealing them. This is just more stress and that is not easier.

Many people simplify their lives after they have been through a trauma of some kind. When I had my near-death experience, I soon sold my house, moved to a small town, opened a small business and had the best time of my life. There was very little stress on me and I enjoyed the freedom.

Even after I sold my business and moved, I tried to make sure my life stayed simpler. It's difficult at times but getting back to nature and listening to my inner self helps keep me there.

Vacations are an example of how we create our own stress. All of us have taken a vacation and rushed around to get ready to go, rushed the whole time we were away because we wanted to see everything, rushed home because we had to go to work the next day and rushed through work because we had been on vacation and the work piled up. STOP!

No matter how you rush around and do things, there will always be things to do. We need to learn how to slow down. Slowing down means you are enjoying the moment more and not thinking about the future and the stress it might bring you. We look too much at what might happen instead of looking at what is happening.

We should also try to remember that problems are just events in the present moment that we have put off. If we don't live in the present moment, we can't see that we are putting things off until later, which in many cases causes problems or a stressful situation. When we slow down and see what is happening right now instead of what might happen, we can handle these events and save ourselves problems in the future.

When it comes to a belief system, make it simple. All the great teachers of the world have all said the same thing, "Make it simple and let go of what you don't need."

It's just like having a storage shed full of junk we never use. Why do we keep paying the bill to have it in storage? What a waste!

If we're storing old beliefs patterns or even someone else's beliefs in our body, mind or soul, we don't have room for our own beliefs. The Universe is in constant change and growth. We should be like that. Change and grow with what you learn about yourself or religion or spirituality, but make it simple.

When people start a new path in life, they read and study and want to learn everything about it. They read someone else's thoughts and words. They learn what someone else believes. Many times they take this information as the only truth. They try to believe the same way the other person believes. That never works. We need to take the information we read and adapt it to our lives and our thoughts.

No one can live or believe exactly like someone else because they aren't that person. So no matter how much they read and learn, they will get different thoughts and ideas on the same thing. This can make learning or believing in something stressful or even impossible for some people. They need to remember that no one will think the same about the same information.

Our belief is our belief. We are in it with our self. We shouldn't need others to be in it with us or believe like we do. If you need that kind of support, you need to look deep inside yourself and try to heal the fear of not being able to believe in yourself.

Letting go of everything doesn't mean sell everything and go live in a cave. It means get rid of the emotion attachment to it. It means to look at the toys and things you have in your life and know they don't mean that much to you. You can enjoy them but the important thing is you.

Toys may be the outer visual affect of what we are feeling on the inside but they aren't us.

Emotions are what we need to experience, feel and then let go of them everyday. When we learn to step back from our emotions, look at how and why they make us feel a certain way, we can then let go of them. They are the toys of our soul, so to speak.

Letting go of emotions we don't need is the best thing you can do for yourself to help simplify your life. Drama is not what you want in your life everyday. Drama is not simplifying your life. It's adding extra ingredients you don't need.

In many beliefs systems you have to worry if you are doing the right thing and if you are pissing off a god. In spirituality, you do what you know is right because everything you do will come back to you in some way. It's not a sin and you won't go to hell, but if you intentionally do something mean or hateful to another person or animal, you will get something mean or hateful back.

In spirituality, you have to take responsibility for your actions, thoughts and words. In many religions, you don't. In many religions you say a prayer and have to do a penance for forgiveness. It seems that each penance is different for each sin, but a thousand "Hail Mary's" still doesn't make it right. There will still be karma to pay.

Religions say "ask for forgiveness and it will be given" and it will, after you get back the karma you put out. Karma rules the Universe and there's no way to get around it or out of its way. You can lessen its affects by asking for grace, taking responsibility for what you did wrong and then don't do it again. That will help.

There are many people who go to church and pray and then don't understand why some bad or uncomfortable things happen to them. They blame God for not listening or not forgiving them. It has nothing to do with God – it has to do with the rules of the Universe.

Praying for forgiveness will help, as long as you really mean it, but the karmic affect of "what you put out you get back" will still have to play itself out. You will still get some uncomfortable things back because of what you put out in your past. If you start today to take responsibility for you and everything about you, you will start putting out positive energy and it will be returned to you.

In spirituality, you don't have to ask for forgiveness, you ask for grace. If you do something that was not of good intent, ask for grace so the karma that comes back to you won't be so harmful. Then don't do the action or thought again. In spirituality, the only way to grow is to learn from your mistakes as you take responsibility for them. If everyone on the planet did this, we would be living in peace and love.

Life is supposed to be simple – it's supposed to be easy. We have made it so complicated it's no fun anymore. We have placed judgments on everything and everyone. Simple means look at life like we were all children again. Can you remember back then?

We accepted people for who they were, not what they had. We laughed, loved and ran free. We were still unsure about what tomorrow would bring but we didn't care either. We knew no matter what came our way we could handle it or walk away from it without the need to get mad or to make someone else feel badly.

If we somehow knew everything would be okay with us no matter what anyone else was doing, it would sure take a lot of stress off of us. But then you ask, "Aren't we supposed to care? Aren't we supposed to help each other?"

The answer is yes but we have to understand one very important thing; everyone is on their path and they have chosen this path long before they came to Earth. These souls wanted or needed to experience what they are experiencing to help them in some way. Remember we all come from a place of love so we need to experience something else.

I think we are all looking for love so much when we are here because of what we have when we are in our energy body on the other side. When we die, it's great but there are some things we can't experience in that dimension.

In this dimension, when we do something wrong and never get caught, we think we are getting away with something. Well, think again. The universal energy knows everything. The energy you put out with any deed, good or bad, will come back. There is no getting around it.

We can help each other by sending love, not judgment to everyone. If we see a wrong, try to right it. If someone is starving and we have plenty, share it. We are all in this together and it's time to understand that. What happens in one country affects us all. What happens in your world will affect someone else's world. Your actions will affect someone, something, some place. This has already been proven.

Just imagine if everyone on the planet really believed that what they put out, they got back! Imagine if everyone knew they were creating karma with bad actions and thoughts and words and it would come back to them. Imagine if everyone believed that we all came from the same Source and that Source was a loving energy that didn't judge us but did let us know we have to be responsible for our own actions, thoughts and words.

We see karma happening everyday, so why are we so blind to it. When someone murders someone, they usually get caught. If they don't, their prison will be bad events happening to them the rest of their lives. Or they will never really be at rest because they will always be looking over their shoulder. Or they might die a very violent death themselves. All these things are karma coming back to them.

We see people who have judged others becoming judged themselves. That's karma. We see people who gossip about others being gossiped about. We see mean people who have major health problems. There are all kinds of karma. I not saying all diseases or conditions that happen to us is karma, but many are.

Many of our own diseases are brought on by our selves. When I say that I mean look at what you are eating, drinking, and smoking. Look at how much you worry and what that does to your stomach as well as the stress lines on your face. How much time do we spend in the sun or the extreme cold? How much anger do we keep inside? How much joy are we hiding?

All these things can and do affect our health, looks and attitude. The energy around them can sit in our bodies and affect the healthy living cells. We can kill our own health just by being negative all the time.

There are all kinds of experiments right now that science is doing to show that just the word "love" or the word "hate" taped to a glass of water changes the way the molecules in the water react. It's an amazing experiment and we should not ignore it. The energy and power of words and thoughts are as real as you are. If science was our religion, we would know this by now.

However, even if we knew this, some of us wouldn't believe it and that's okay. Some of us just have to learn things the hard way and that's okay too. That's who we are and what we do. However if we can look at our situations as a result of past choices, we can learn to change our patterns of self abuse and sabotage.

The Universe will put us in uncomfortable situations so we can learn and grow. It takes us out of our comfort zone so we can see what we need to do to help ourselves. Once we see what has to be done, we can walk through it, knowing everything will be okay in the end.

A simple belief system takes much of the drama, trauma and unrest out of your life. So many of us are afraid of "sinning" because we'll go to hell, it's just not funny anymore.

It's almost impossible to keep track of what's a sin and what's not a sin anymore. Are too many tattoos a sin? Are wearing baggy pants a sin? Is the "wrong" hair cut a sin? Is looking one way a sin compared to looking another?

There are over 6200 religions around the world; which one is the right one? Which one should be the "one" to tell us what is right or what is wrong? Each of these 6200 religions have their own belief system and their own rules and their own sins. If we believed in just half them, we'd all be afraid of doing anything because I'm sure it would be a sin somewhere.

Many people think you have to "pick" a religion to go to heaven or be "saved". Well, out of 6200 religions around the world, picking the right one is like winning the lottery. What if the religion you pick is somehow the "wrong" religion and the gods send you to hell anyway.

Spirituality says, "Take care of your self and everything else will fall into place". Spirituality says you don't need to "join" anything. Think and do loving thoughts and actions toward others. Acts of kindness at all times to people and animals and plants will bring you acts of kindness. Good intentions will bring forth good deeds. Believing you are part of the greater good and a greater power is a good thing.

Knowing you are a "god" in yourself and using that godliness for only good, not revenge or out of anger, is what we are here to do. Knowing that we can manifest anything we want to – good or evil. Knowing that the cycle of life is just that – live, learn, grow and die. Die to go home and rest and learn some more.

Life is a simple game we play to experience what we can't experience on the other side. Life is what we experience and see every day. We see the birth, life and death of animals, trees and plants and even galaxies and solar systems. Everything in this world and the worlds beyond have the same patterns. Only our souls live forever and ever. Yet they go through a birth and death every time we come back to Earth in a reincarnation. They go through a birth and death every time we go to another solar system and experience what we are supposed to experience there.

When we let go of the dogma of old patterns that aren't serving us anymore, we free our soul to walk into new ideals and new energy that will service us. I just shake my head when people tell me their life isn't working anymore, yet they don't know what to do to change it. Well, you do whatever you have to do to change it.

You look at the fear that is holding you back and you laugh at it. Religions, groups, cults, memberships, gangs, the gathering of people and society as a whole all tend to want to control the people in that group. In every group there are leaders and there are followers. We need to get to a point where we are all leaders of our own life and destiny. We don't need to follow or copy anyone because we will never be "them".

All we need to do is join our self in our own highest good. We can be our own group and groupie! We really don't NEED anyone. It's nice to have someone in our lives to share our stuff with but we don't need someone to make us whole. We come into this life on our own and we go out on our own. Life is a simple game of choices and experiences from those choices. Fear shouldn't be one of those choices.

I've walked out of many things in my life that weren't working for me and each time I've found something better. I'm not attached to many things so they don't hold me back. I can move to another town, state or anywhere in a week and never regret it. I can let go of everything in this world that is material and it doesn't bother me. I try to see the light and goodness in everything. I try not to judge anyone or anything because I know people will get their karma back and events are unfolding the way they are supposed to unfold.

My belief systems is that this world is perfect just the way it is because it's teaching us how we are supposed to live and change. There isn't one thing out of place or wrong. Everything is happening just like its supposed to. If the Universe has run itself for over 12 billion years without our help, what makes us think it needs it now? We're the ones that have messed it up, but it will heal itself with or without our help.

There is a master plan and it's simple. "Everything is being taken care of". That means from the smallest insect to the largest mammal. Nothing is being ignored, over-looked, misunderstood, un-noticed or left out. Nothing is unimportant. Everything is how it's supposed to be.

Species of animals will come and go so they can adapt to the changes happening on Mother Earth. Hell, even humans have changed to meet the evolution that is a constant happening on Earth. We aren't what we were even 100 years ago.

Life is supposed to be looked at through the eyes of a child. It's supposed to be new everyday with different things to discover. It's supposed to be joyful, not filled with fear of pissing off a god.

The one question I've always had about "a loving God" is why do we have to fear Him? If he's so all powerful and loving, why would he allow us to burn in hell? Wouldn't he just give us a good talking to and let us learn on our own. If he gave us free will to make our own choices, why would he punish us for doing it? Religion just doesn't make sense to me.

Just make it simple and don't over analyze it. Believe what feels right to you. Love everything but don't get attached to it or the outcome of anything. Look for good in everything and you will see it. Know that everything is just how it's supposed to be at all times. If a situation is uncomfortable to you, look to see what you are learning and how you can walk through it with grace. Love yourself so you can love others.

This is how life should be. This is what it started out like. Stop the trauma, drama and fear of being wrong, doing wrong and going to hell. Live in joy, peace and love and that's what you'll get back. Flow with changes and just make it simple!